MUSEUM architecture

ACKNOWLEDGMENTS

First, thanks to Donna Day, wife, lover, best friend.

Thanks to Rockport Publishers, and especially acquisitions editor Rosalie Grattaroti and editor Martha Wetherill, for supporting my efforts and for helping make possible the appearance of this book.

Thanks to the charming and invariably good-humored Arthur Rosenblatt, who not only wrote the fine foreword to the book but also, in several conversations, subtly steered me into new ways of thinking about museum architecture.

The most intractable problem in writing the book was a shortage of time and resources that prevented me from visiting every museum included herein. Instead, in many instances I looked at pictures and read texts provided by architects; I also read articles in magazines. I would like to thank the architectural writers—both editorial and in-house at architectural firms—whose efforts predated mine. Your articles, press releases, and design narratives were invaluable to me in writing my own essays.

Also thanks to the photographers whose brilliant work brings these pages to life. Above all, thanks to all the visionary architects and their formidable design teams for making these memorable buildings.

First published in the United States of America by

Rockport Publishers, Inc.
33 Commercial Street
Gloucester, Massachusetts 01930-5089
Telephone: (978) 282-9590
Facsimile: (978) 283-2742

ISBN 1 84000 095 3

Design: Wren Design

Front cover image: Ehime Prefectural Museum of General Science, Ehime, Japan; Kisho Kurokawa Architect & Associates. Photo by Tomio Ohashi.

Back cover images: (top and bottom right) Art Gallery of Ontario, Toronto, Ontario, Canada; Barton Myers Associates, Inc. Photo by Steven Evans. (center) Ehime Prefectural Museum of General Science. Photo by Tomio Ohashi.

Front flap image: Ehime Prefectural Museum of General Science. Photo by Tomio Ohashi.

Back flap images: Photo of author by Donna Day. Photo of Arthur Rosenblatt, FAIA, by Stan Reis Photography.

Interior page images: (page 4) Whanki Museum, Kyu Sung Woo Architect, photo by Timothy Hursley; (page 6) Arizona Science Center, Antoine Predock Architect, photo by Timothy Hursley; (page 8) San Francisco Museum of Modern Art, Mario Botta Architetto, photo by Richard Barnes; (page 10) Ehime Prefectural Museum of General Science, Kisho Kurokawa Architect & Associates, photo by Tomio Ohashi; (page 12) Guggenheim Museum Bilbao, Frank O. Gehry and Associates, photo by Donna Day; (page 192) photo of author by Donna Day.

Manufactured in china

MUSEUM architecture

Justin Henderson

MITCHELL BEAZLEY

CONTENTS

FOREWORD

Arthur Rosenblatt, FAIA

Unlike any other structure, the museum is a singular building type, a coveted commission for an architect. Because of its position as a manifestation of intense public pride, it is subject to the most critical scrutiny. The museum clearly exposes the constant tension between the specialized need of the institution, its unique requirements for exhibition, preservation, and education, and the desire of the architect for an aesthetic statement. It can be an important achievement that determines the success or failure of the architect's career.

New and expanded museums are invariably the most architecturally interesting buildings and attract the most talented and innovative architects. This book provides a world overview of museum architecture today. It is a state-of-the-art account of contemporary museums from a design point of view.

The museum has its origins in the late eighteenth and early nineteenth centuries. Among the first public museums were the Capitoline Museum in Rome (1734), the Vatican's Museo Pio Clementino in the late eighteenth century, and the Musee du Louvre in Paris, which actually was never designed to be a museum. Originally a medieval fortress, it was located at a point where the Paris defenses of A.D. 1200 were weakest.

The earliest museums were not a distinct building type and rarely were architects called upon to develop a distinct programmatic form. However, the appearance of Jean-Nicolas-Louis Durand's *Précis des Leçons d'Architecture Données à l'Ecole Polytechnique* (Paris, 1802–1805) as a specific design for a museum building type, with an emphasis on the utilitarian, had a profound effect on the architect's role in the design of this new kind of structure.

Sir John Soane's Dulwich Gallery in London (1811–1814) and Karl Friedrich Schinkel's Altes Museum in Berlin (1823–1830) reflect Durand's concerns for program and functional requirements, and both represent the most notable early examples of an architect's design of an edifice specifically with a public museum role. Schinkel's Altes Museum represents another significant change: it was conceived as more than a place in which exhibits could be housed and the public could be educated. It was part of a greater scheme of civic improvement and thus further expanded the role of the museum structure in society. The museum, therefore, becomes more than a vehicle for the exhibition, study, and preservation of precious objects; it represents the highest goals and aspirations of a society and, even more importantly, becomes a bold statement of civic and national pride. In fact, I. M. Pei's brilliant consolidation and completion of the Louvre (Paris, 1993) was an additional political expression of President Mitterand and his belief in France's leadership in the arts.

The last decade has seen an extraordinary acceleration in the number of new and expanded existing museums throughout the world. Museums in different societies have distinct origins and there is no simple pattern to their development. While pride is a constant theme in

the institutions described in this volume, their initial development is generated by an endless variety of factors. Many have been spawned by existing civic and national collections. In some instances, particularly in Japan and Switzerland, private corporations, intent on advancing their presence in society, have initiated and funded new institutions. Some projects reflect an interest in increasing tourism; other larger ones are bent on decentralizing and opening branches in other countries, which is best illustrated by New York's Guggenheim Museum's outreach into Spain, Germany, and Italy.

This book also reveals a surprising increase in the variety of subjects housed in the "new museum." In addition to the more traditional interests in art and sculpture, a large number are devoted to history, science, computer technology, music, and entertainment. Environmental concerns are also evident, with the emphasis on controlling energy consumption and building with less wasteful materials. And an entirely new awareness and interest is shown in the protection and preservation of collections; the most innovative efforts are being made to maintain public accessibility while simultaneously ensuring the safekeeping of the collections.

As the founding director of the United States Holocaust Memorial Museum in Washington, D.C., I am particularly pleased that this volume includes this important institution. The sensitive design by James Ingo Freed illustrates how architecture can be both evocative and moving in the development of a "storytelling" museum of history.

In assessing the success of the architects in the museum designs illustrated in this book, it should be emphasized that architectural quality is of course primarily, but not limited to, aesthetic quality. The work of architecture is the product of function and art. The architectural historian, Nicholas Pevner, noted that ". . . the guardian of functional satisfaction is the client. His responsibility in briefing is as great as the architect's in designing."

Arthur Rosenblatt served as the founding director of the United States Holocaust Memorial Museum in Washington, D.C., and was for nineteen years, both vice president and vice director of the Metropolitan Museum of Art. Currently he is senior principal of RKK&G, Museum and Cultural Facilities Consultants, Inc., a New York City-based office offering museum-planning and design services worldwide. He is the recipient of the American Institute of Architects' 1998 Thomas Jefferson Award for Public Architecture.

INTRODUCTION

A GOLDEN AGE OF MUSEUM ARCHITECTURE

Even a casual review of *Museum Architecture* reveals that museum building in the 1990s is booming, and that architects play a critical role. Whether they are designed by international superstar architects or respected regional or national firms, museums consistently rank among the most original, intriguing, and challenging buildings designed in the world today.

"Booming" as a description may send a mixed message, which seems appropriate in the world of museum design. The blockbuster mentality of pop culture, in movies, television, and best sellers, has seeped into the museum world as well. Many of the new museums are made to handle large crowds, and, to attract those crowds, these buildings are often made to draw attention to themselves. Museums have always been cultural and research centers, but now they additionally serve as social gathering places, educational resources, and marketing meccas: just about every new art museum designed today contains a strategically situated store, and many have elegant dining rooms and/or jazzy new cafes as well. Movie theaters, stages, multimedia facilities, and other spots to congregate are also part of the mix, as museum designers and directors seek to maximize their appeal to the public.

Museum commissions are well loved by architects, for in designing museums, architects are encouraged to be inventive in ways unimaginable when designing an office building or other large-scale project. Museum programming has its functional complexities, but above all it cries out for originality of design. Nobody goes to a museum from nine to five, wearing a suit and watching the clock. They go for education, enlightenment, stories, culture, thrills. They want, and expect, to be intrigued by the architecture as well as the art and artifacts. Museums provide architects with opportunities to be both innovative and entertaining. If the entertaining quality occasionally leans toward gimmickry, even that is preferable to sterility.

The objects on display in the museums herein range from traditional artworks and artifacts to the decidedly offbeat. Some of the buildings featured in this book contain, among other collections: the contents of the tombs of dead emperors; road signs and fast cars; the eccentric holdings, in a dozen different fields, of a single, wealthy patron; and artworks of the twentieth century or the last twenty centuries. A personal collection of chairs fills one museum, while another narrates the story of the most devastating historical event of the modern era, the Holocaust.

Architects approach the making of these buildings in myriad ways. At times, the collections dictate the form of the building: at Chikatsu-Asuka, a historical museum by Tadao Ando preserves and displays artifacts from a series of burial mounds constructed in Japan over a thousand years ago. Reflecting the contents, the museum itself is designed like a tomb, with much of its interior buried underground. In Mexico City, Ricardo Legoretta's Papalote Children's Museum is a playful essay in bright, lively color and simple geometry, designed to appeal to children. The Route 66 Museum

sports a neon glow like a roadhouse or a motel. In other words, form often follows not function but content.

On the other hand, when an innovator such as Frank Gehry is unleashed on a contemporary art museum project, a building results that is as much sculpture as art container. At Bilbao, Spain, Gehry has made a Guggenheim Museum that extends the notion of the contemporary museum into a new realm. This building is surely as challenging as anything that will go inside it. In Bilbao, form is content.

Other, more restrained architects such as Richard Meier and Mario Botta have also created memorable art museums whose distinctly different yet equally monumental styles accurately reflect their contexts—a hilly, low-rise L.A. suburb, a busy urban neighborhood not far from downtown San Francisco—as well as their contents.

The organization of the book into three sections, General-Interest Art Museums, Specialized Art Museums, and Other Museums, reflects the widespread dissemination of creative museum-building into cultural realms far beyond the predictable art and natural-history realms of the past. There have always been smaller museums devoted to quirky or obscure subject matter, but historically they have not been housed in architecturally significant buildings, such as Gehry's Vitra Design Museum or the Ehime Prefectural Museum of General Science by Kisho Kurokawa.

General-Interest Art Museums here refers to museums like the Guggenheim Bilbao or the Art Gallery of Toronto that offer more than the work of one artist or genre; Specialized Art Museums, on the other hand, focus on a single artist—Warhol, Whanki—or a specialized or seemingly exotic artistic genre. The Museum for African Art in New York City, for example, focuses on African art and craft, less understood or appreciated by Westerners, whereas the Shiga Kogen Roman Art Museum in Japan offers a stunningly displayed collection of ancient-Roman glass—a foreign subject, certainly, to the Japanese. As a third category, Other Museums included here contains everything else: historical artifacts, planetariums, chairs, cars, all manner of items people considered worthy of collecting.

Not everyone cares to know the detailed history of an American highway, as is wittily narrated at the Route 66 Museum in Clinton, Oklahoma; nor have the figurative works of nineteenth-century German painters that dominate the collection in Seattle's Frye Museum generated strong interest in the art world—but the new or renovated buildings that house these collections are marvelous additions to their respective landscapes. The built environment, cluttered with a surfeit of bland, at times mediocre structures, can only be improved as museums proliferate around the world. Some proof of that can be found in the work shown on the pages that follow.

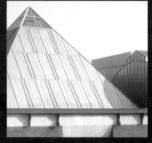

GENERAL-INTEREST
art museums

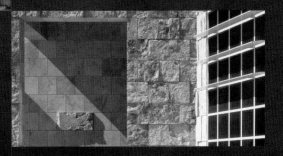

SCULPTED BY NATURE

A museum that is also a hotel, this exquisite architectural hybrid was designed by Japanese architect Tadao Ando on a site within a national park on the island of Naoshima. The buildings are positioned on a grassy bluff at the southern tip of the island, overlooking the beach and surf below. Approach to the museum is by water, so its design is oriented to the sea and the pier.

Leaving the wharf, visitors encounter a small, stepped plaza that serves as the museum entrance. Here also is a small, underground annex. Intersecting stone-and-concrete forms of the low-rise museum

exterior—simple planes, curves, and cylinders, in muted natural tones—emerge into view during the ascent on the plaza steps.

Yet, scarcely half of the museum's volume is visible, for much of it is buried underground to minimize intrusion on the serene natural setting. On entering the main building, visitors soon find themselves in a surprisingly expansive volume—a double height underground gallery nearly 150 feet long (45.7 meters long) and 25 feet wide (7.6 meters wide). This rectangular space is intersected by a cylindrical gallery rising from the basement level. An oculus capping the cylinder is enclosed beneath a glass

Arriving at the Naoshima Contemporary Art Museum, visitors disembark at the pier, then ascend to the terrace near the lower annex. Seen from there, the museum emerges from the hillside as a quiet assemblage of simple forms and muted colors. The peaked glass cone admits light into the heart of the half-buried building.

Photos by Mitsuo Matsuoka

Joining the building to the landscape, Ando demonstrates that the elemental forms and colors of earth, sky, and sea make compelling backdrops for modern artworks, especially when these backdrops are executed in natural building materials, or shaped and framed by the hand of a master.

Photos by Mitsuo Matsuoka

cone, admitting daylight deep into the interior. Hotel guestrooms occupy two stories of a stone-clad rectangular block resting diagonally atop the primary volume. The building is open to the sky and sea; and thus the views become part of the architecture, while the architecture, in the manner of site-specific sculpture, becomes an integral part of the landscape.

Several years after completing the initial museum/hotel complex, Ando designed another hybrid gallery/hotel structure on the hill, 100 feet (30.5 meters) above the original. A cable car and a network of trails link the freestanding annex to the main structure.

The annex is an oval-shaped, single-story structure, and like the original museum, pierces the hillside. A cafeteria, offices, and more guest rooms are located within the annex, and wrap around a central water feature— a still, oval-shaped pool—surrounded by a colonnade used for outdoor gallery space. The entrance to the annex is marked with a waterfall and a garden between the oval and an L-shaped wall. The new building, like the original museum and entry plaza, is deeply enmeshed in its landscape. The strong, quiet forms of these structures are striking, serene yet dramatic, timeless in their relationship to the primeval setting.

Much of the museum's volume is virtually buried in the hillside site, providing a dramatic experience for the visitor coming in from outside to discover spacious galleries bathed in natural light— or darkened to enhance the effect of the neon text piece. Allowing the artworks so much space to breathe enhances their power.

Photos by Mitsuo Matsuoka

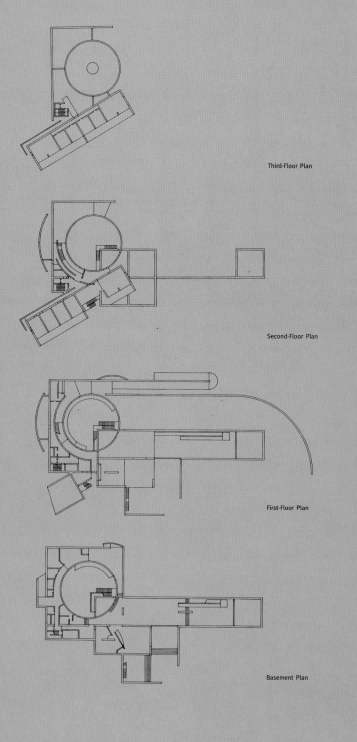

Third-Floor Plan

Second-Floor Plan

First-Floor Plan

Basement Plan

Plans of the main museum's four floors show the intersection of assorted volumes on differing levels. The cylindrical gallery begins at the basement (lower left) and rises through the building to the roof, while the rectangular galleries are stacked on several levels, and the two floors of the small hotel wing rest atop the building's primary volume.

With the Inland Sea and neighboring islands visible in the distance, the museum is at left, the guest-room wing at right. The architect celebrates and respects the site's beauty by staying close to the ground, allowing the setting rather than the building to dominate.

Photo by Mitsuo Matsuoka

Site plan shows the wharf and entrance terrace at left, the main building at center, and the annex addition with guest rooms and galleries at the top of the hill to the right.

Photo by Tadao Ando

The oval-shaped annex surrounds
a central water feature. Rooftop
plantings knit this structure deeply
into the landscape, while the
waterfall contained between the
oval and a stone perimeter wall
makes a visceral connection with
the sea.

Photos by Tomio Ohashi

Art Gallery of Ontario
Toronto, Ontario, Canada
Barton Myers Associates, Inc.
Joint Venture with Kuwabara Payne McKenna Blumberg Architects

CONTEXTUAL UNITY
FROM URBAN DIVERSITY

One of the world's more civic-minded cities, Toronto is graced with a strong urban character and a diverse ethnic populace. Two centuries of history are reflected in the buildings that comprise the city fabric.

The Art Gallery of Ontario (AGO) embodies much of the city's design history. By the time Los Angeles-based Barton Myers Architect, Inc. (in joint venture with local Kuwabara Payne McKenna Blumberg Architects) won the commission to renovate and expand the AGO in the 1980s, the institution had experienced nearly a century of growth, sprawling amidst a jumble of nineteenth- and twentieth-century buildings of differing architectural styles.

For a museum, this sort of random growth has its drawbacks, as additions and expansions here and there can eventually lead to missed opportunities and failed strategies. Along with stylistic clashes, there were major circulation problems, such as grand stairs leading to basement rest rooms and service entrances where logic begged for large-scale foyers. Beyond aesthetic improvements and additional galleries, the expansion was necessary to create space for two imperative functions of the modern museum: fundraising and retailing.

The history of the AGO begins with the Grange. Toronto's oldest standing brick house, the Grange served as the museum's first home in 1913. Three Beaux-Arts-style rooms were added to the north of the classically proportioned house in 1918, followed by further expansions in 1925 and 1933. In 1968, sections of the earlier additions were demolished, and the Beaux-Arts building was wrapped in a modern box. A second modernist renovation in 1977 set the stage for Myers.

The Muzzo di Luca Tower and a glass-capped pyramid make a dramatic entry statement on the new north facade of the Art Gallery of Ontario. The horizontal barrel vault encloses second-story galleries, with retail space below.

A glass atrium links the AGO's first two structures—the circa-1817 Grange, just visible through the glass wall at left, with the 1918 Beaux-Arts addition at right. The former exterior wall of the 1918 addition is now an interior wall of the new sculpture court, and its neo-Renaissance detailing provides some warming decoration in this spare, dramatic volume.

All photos by Steven Evans

Festive brick bays and ornamental steel cornices gently decorate the Art Gallery of Ontario's front facade, echoing nearby Victorian houses and attracting passersby on the busy thoroughfare. The glass storefronts provide easy access for shoppers.

In planning his expansion, Myers wisely looked to the urban context of the existing institution. The AGO is hemmed in by unique streets and buildings, each with its own character, and Meyers' museum expansion responds to each accordingly. His plan clarifies circulation, celebrates the building's multifaceted history, and adds about 100,000 square feet (9,000 square meters) of space in thirty new and twenty renovated galleries.

On its north side, the AGO fronts the Victorian brick houses of busy Dundas Street. Here, Myers created a bayed brick-and-sandstone facade with steel cornices to match neighboring historic houses. Behind this facade, a new barrel vault rises over a series of second-floor galleries of contemporary art. New glass storefronts connect with the street on the ground floor. At the east end of the new facade, a pyramid detailed with light slots announces the new north side-entry court, and an adjacent 105-foot (32-meter) tower makes a vertical counterpoint to the horizontal stretch of the barrel vault. Together, they clarify the museum's primary entrance and raise its street presence.

Myers' challenge on the south side was to link the original two-story building with the 1925 Beaux-Arts addition, integrating both with the adjacent new construction that houses a library and museum offices. Myers diminished the mass of the new structures with setbacks, using rooflines, window openings, and other elements to echo period details of earlier structures. Enclosing the space between the early buildings beneath a glass roof, the architect created a spacious, daylit sculpture court. The grand volume of the atrium is scaled down by the rich, Renaissance Revival detail of the limestone wall of the 1925 addition—a wall propitiously "moved" from the outside in when the roof was added.

Some might view the updated AGO as lacking unity, but the complex assemblage of new and renovated volumes reflects, and thus enhances, its mixed urban context and evolution. Or, as Myers says, "It all hangs together like the disparate parts of a city."

From one end of the vast, labyrinthine building to the other, the existing and new exhibition galleries have been designed, modernized, or restored in styles true to their own histories or collections. This elegantly conceived and executed expansion moves the Art Gallery of Ontario into the top ranks of museums worldwide.

The south facade includes the circa-1817 house, the Grange Building, AGO's home since 1913. Setting back the bulk of the new Chalmers Wing lessens the impact of its mass. The wing's peaked glass roof (behind the Grange), along with its brick finish and complementary forms, link it with the 1918 Beaux-Arts addition and enclose the new Tanenbaum Sculpture Atrium.

The spacious new lobby is graced by a pyramid-shaped roof with neo-Egyptian light slots. One of the museum's prized possessions, the original plaster cast for Henry Moore's Draped Reclining Figure, is framed in an opening to the new east-west circulation spine. On the floor, Michael Simon's Walking Woman.

New and renovated galleries are devoid of ornamentation to prevent competition with the museum's collection of contemporary paintings and sculpture.

The new east-west spine establishes clear circulation, as seen in the gallery enfilade. Warm woods mark transition points, but gallery spaces for contemporary works have been kept sparse and white.

Articulated windows provide daylight to library spaces and establish a graceful transition between vertical walls and the curve of the ceiling vault. Uplighting defines the structure and helps prevent glare.

A beautifully detailed metal spiral stair leading to the upper level galleries provides the drama of a grand staircase without occupying vast amounts of space. Suspended track lighting focuses on sculpted Inuit pieces in a barrel-vaulted gallery that was claimed from former administrative office space.

Renovated galleries in the older buildings exhibit more traditional Canadian artworks. They are residentially scaled, and painted in warm, intimate colors in keeping with the genre on display.

A MASTERPIECE FOR THE MILLENNIUM

Without a doubt Frank Gehry's new Guggenheim Museum Bilbao is destined to take its place among the architectural masterworks of the twentieth century. Located in Bilbao, an industrial city in the Basque province of northern Spain, the Guggenheim Bilbao is the most strikingly original building of this scale that has been built anywhere in the world in this decade (another Guggenheim, its form echoed here, comes to mind as perhaps the only legitimate precursor). And yet, for all its iconoclastic energy, the museum sits comfortably in gritty, industrial terrain surrounded by aging buildings, railyards, bridges, and the waters of the Nervion River.

The primary exterior finish materials are titanium, limestone, and glass. The brilliant interplay of metal and stone, transparency and opacity, grounded, blocky geometry and explosive free-form sculpture is astonishingly daring and graceful. Every perspective provides a new revelation. The enchanting, careening cubist artichoke seen from the bridge is transformed into a long, gracefully abstracted boat when viewed from across the river. One moment the sun ignites the voluptuous arrangement of tumbling titanium cubes in a molten flare; the next it goes behind a cloud, and the skin of the building goes soft and satiny, absorptive, contemplative.

All photos by Donna Day

Located in the industrial city of Bilbao (Spain's fourth largest city), the building is contained on four sides by a railyard, a road, a bridge, and a river. The near surroundings are industrial, but there are green hills in the distance, and they form part of the composition as well. A selection of photographs taken during a 360-degree hike around the site—a hike encompassing two bridges and two roadways—puts the building into context and shows how shifting perspectives reveal its voluptuous, multi-faceted character.

Organized around a central atrium more than 163 feet high (50 meters high) and ringed with an interwoven system of glass elevators, bridges, and stair towers, the interior galleries range from square, sequentially arranged spaces meant to house permanent collections to the sinuously curving volume of the "boat" gallery, designed for temporary exhibitions. These vast, at times unpredictable, galleries present artists with a new kind of challenge: making art good enough, or large enough, or powerful enough, to not get lost in the space.

There are signs of ongoing exterior construction in these photographs taken prior to the museum's opening, but in this rough, urban, riverfront site it is likely that the building will always be surrounded by machinery, boats, trains, cars, the trappings of urban industrial reality. Gehry has taken that reality as the basis for a building that is as challenging, distinct, and beautiful as anything an artist might put inside it.

MARCO Contemporary Art Museum
Monterrey, Mexico
Legorreta Arquitectos

THE CLARITY OF MEXICAN MODERNISM

Ricardo Legorreta's striking two-story contemporary art museum in the northern Mexican city of Monterrey takes the traditional plan of the Mexican house as its fundamental ordering scheme, with a square central courtyard framed by an arcade that provides access to adjacent rooms— or in this case, galleries. Located on a busy corner of Monterrey's central plaza close to the city's main cathedral, the museum, like many of Legorreta's buildings, also owes a debt of influence to the work of the great Mexican architect Luis Barragán. Yet there's a big difference: Barragán primarily worked on a small scale, in the residential mode. Legorreta's more ambitious architecture—hotels, office buildings, and museums like MARCO—expands Barragán's austere geometries of intersecting planes, elegant water features, and still, sacred spaces onto a larger, more public stage.

Legorreta makes a public nod to Barragán in the museum's entry plaza, where a large sculpture of a dove by Juan Soriano pays homage to Barragán's pigeon house. Carved out of a corner of the plaster-finished building of terra-cotta tones, the entry plaza provides a graceful transition from the street to the interior. The extroverted position of the entry plaza is useful for this public institution; in spite of its windows and openings, the building is essentially introverted, oriented to the courtyard at its heart like many classic Mexican and Spanish structures.

The centrally located courtyard is the heart of the building. The space plan, with galleries and other volumes accessed from an arcade surrounding the inner courtyard, derives from the floorplan of the traditional Mexican house. Water flows in *from an opening in the wall containing the stairwell. Generous windows and doors allow visual contact with the surrounding galleries, while skylights in the high ceiling wash the space with great amounts of daylight.*

The entry plaza is graced with an enormous dove sculpted by Juan Soriano—an homage to Luis Barragán, the great Mexican architect who has had a significant influence on Legorreta. A glowing yellow arcade with purple columns is typical of the bold color highlights employed by the architect to counterpoint the understated interior and exterior colors.

All photos by Lourdes Legorreta

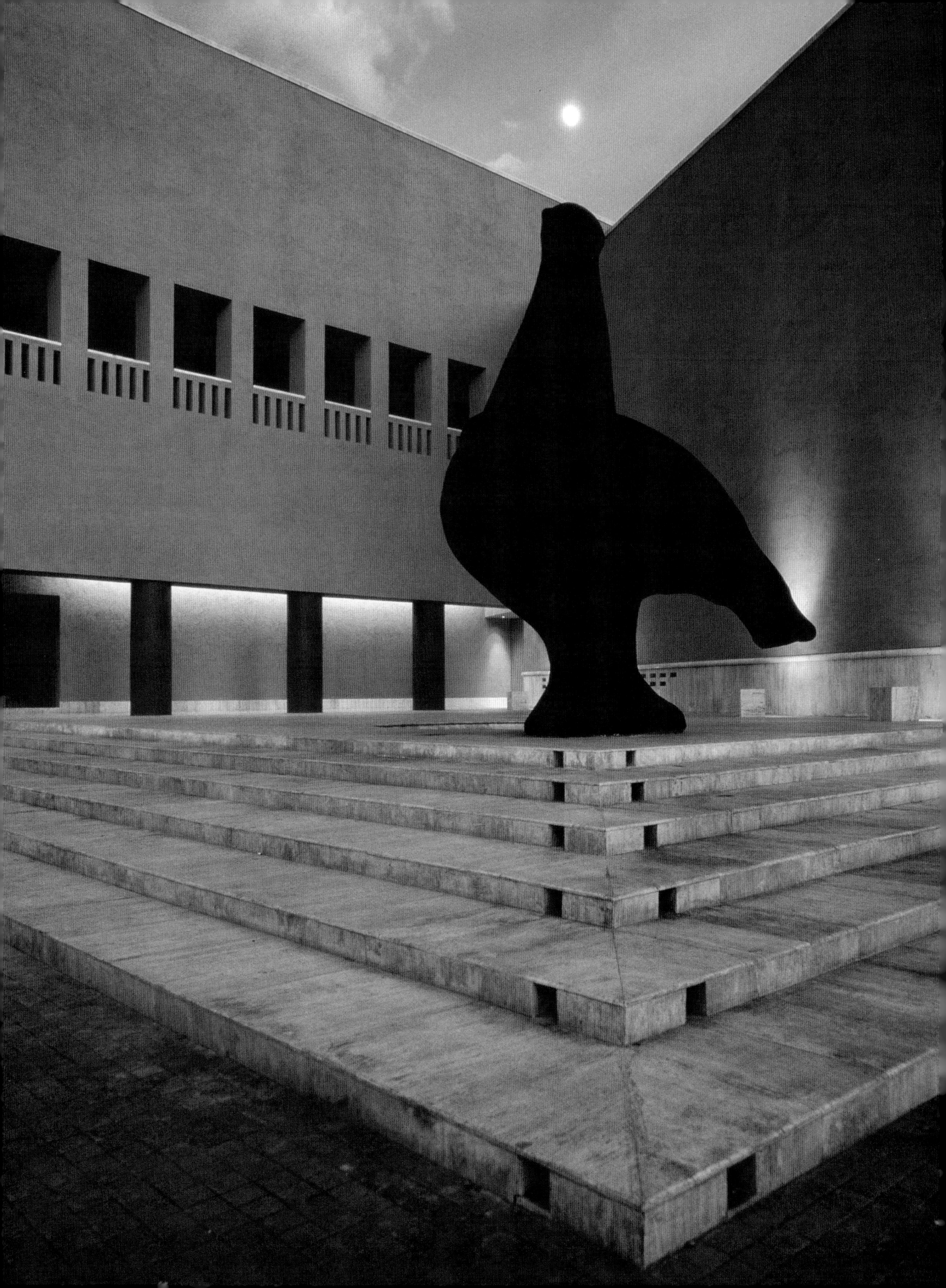

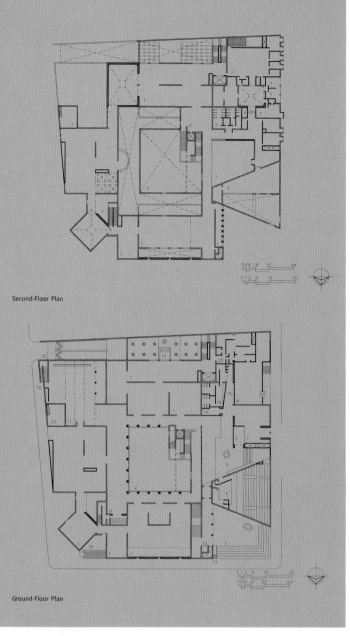

Second-Floor Plan

Ground-Floor Plan

Plans of the first and second floors, with entry plaza at lower right. Galleries wrap around a central courtyard in a floorplan based on that of the traditional Mexican house.

From the plaza, a pair of inconspicuous doors accesses a high-ceilinged vestibule washed with carefully modulated daylight and color. The shift in scale as one passes from the plaza through the small doors into the vestibule heightens the impact of the tall space, dramatically enhancing the simple act of entrance. Immediately accessible from the vestibule are the auditorium, souvenir shop, and cafe.

Sculpted latticework delineates the passage from the vestibule to the double-height main courtyard, the museum's central, primary volume. Bathed in daylight from generously proportioned wall openings and a skylight system, this courtyard is a vibrant, lively space, its primarily neutral surfaces accented with pink and yellow highlights. The center of the marble floor is occupied by a wide, shallow fountain fed by water flowing out of a stairwell wall; the slow trickle occasionally turns to a small torrent, refreshing the room. The floor of the fountain is decorated with multicolored marble tile in circular and semicircular patterns, counterpointing the rectilinear geometry that defines the architecture throughout the interior. In the tradition of the hacienda courtyard, this is a marvelously airy, outdoor space brought indoors.

The arcade surrounding the fountain is bordered by simple rectangular columns extending down from a partial upper wall, their bases wrapped in the same marble as the arcade floor; behind these columns are comfortably furnished seating areas. Paintings are found on the courtyard's perimeter walls and the entrances to the museum's various galleries. The galleries on both ground and upper levels are all diversely proportioned to vary the art-viewing experience, with skylights and other openings providing natural light and strategically situated windows establishing visual connections with the central courtyard and the city beyond.

Legorreta's integration of rough-hewn and fine materials, his subtle use of vibrant colors for interior highlights, and the intermingling of indoor and outdoor spaces all serve to create a building that enriches the experience of viewing the art it contains.

Hot, vibrant colors, used sparingly, can have tremendous impact, as is evident in the pink courtyard (left) and the central courtyard (opposite).

Galleries vary in size and shape throughout the two levels of the museum. Patterned wooden floors make a good textural counterpoint to the spareness of the virtually unadorned walls and openings (opposite). The lighting mixes daylight and artificial light where necessary. The connections between different galleries and the central courtyard enhance the inside/outside quality of the spaces (right).

The building is dignified through geometric clarity, a sense of spatial ordering. The high, angled tower set back from the corner establishes the museum's street presence.

A CATHEDRAL FOR MODERN ART

To better understand Mario Botta's magnificent San Francisco Museum of Modern Art (SFMOMA), examine the architect's own words regarding urban museum design: "In today's city, the museum plays a role analogous to that of the cathedral of yesterday." He considers the museum a modern-day temple, a gathering place where people seek grace. Temple or not, SFMOMA is a powerful building that has completed the transformation of the area of San Francisco known as SOMA, or South of Market (Street). Formerly a skid-row neighborhood, SOMA has recently become a hip, high-tech haven; with the new museum and the arts complex of the Yerba Buena Gardens across the street, it commands the city's cultural landscape.

The architectural element that elevates the tiered, fortress-like, five-story building into a higher realm is the black and silver-striped, angled cylinder at its center—a granite-clad lantern crowned with a glass skylight. The cylinder faintly echoes the smokestacks of industrial cityscapes; more significantly, the glass-topped form evokes the lantern towers that adorn many medieval cathedrals.

All photos by Richard Barnes

A 38-foot-long (11.6-meter-long) bridge crosses the cylindrical light well at the uppermost level, providing museum-goers with a vantage point to float above the atrium (above and previous page). Window slots at the end of the bridge axis provide city views. Shadows and patterns carved into the walls of the light well add visual dynamics to the simplicity of white walls. The small round openings in the wall by the bridge are part of the building's ventilation system.

Without this striped cylinder and its luminous facade, the nearly window-less exterior would be somewhat forbidding, although the elegant brick-work, with angled lines, indented corners, and other flourishes, creates subtle variations of light and shadow on the monochromatic surface. The patterned brick and setbacks lend the museum a graceful presence when seen from a distance; closer in at ground level, the building's mass weighs rather heavily on the understated entrance with its small doors.

The logic behind the modest entry is breathtakingly evident as one passes through the doorways into the grand volume of the atrium, bathed in a wave of daylight pouring through the circular skylight, its highest point at 135 feet (41.2 meters). Organized around three pairs of columns reaching from floor to ceiling, the light-filled atrium serves as an indoor piazza, an Italian-style town center surrounded by lively spaces: a bookstore, a cafe, meeting rooms, a children's art school, and an auditorium placed behind the sculptural double staircase that rises into the cylinder. Also enhancing the atrium's Italianate quality is the selection of materials: the floor is striped with black and dark-gray granite, with the pattern continuing into the staircase. The upper walls and ceilings are finished in maple, shifting to stark white sheetrock for the second and third levels of the atrium, where balconies and stair landings overlook the piazza.

The museum's grand, piazza-like atrium is the heart of the building. Black and gray-striped granite floors are carried up into the dramatic double stair rising into the cylindrical light well.

Surrounding the upper levels of the atrium are four floors of rectangular galleries totaling 50,000 square feet (4,500 square meters), doubling the amount of space the museum had in its original location. Botta designed ceiling systems—"light condensers"—that combine artificial and natural light for the two top floors of temporary exhibition galleries. He also put in a bridge across the upper reaches of the lightwell. Though it hinders the view of the skylight from below, it provides museum-goers with a spectacular vantage point for looking down into the atrium and up into the skylight, with its patterned glass suggestive of a diaphanous leaf. Other views are provided by strategically placed openings in the exterior. On the third story, where drawings and photographs are shown, the lighting is artificial and the ceilings lowered to 12 feet (3.7 meters). The second-floor galleries display the museum's permanent collection of primarily Bay Area and New York School artists, in a series of skylit rooms arranged in an enfilade along a 210-foot (64-meter) axis. These four floors contain the largest collection of galleries for modern and contemporary art on the West Coast.

A church that celebrates creative human endeavor, this splendid and imposing structure will likely outlast most of the skyscrapers that peer down at it from the financial district north of Market Street. Like the cathedrals that indirectly inspired it, the San Francisco Museum of Modern Art is a transcendent building that succeeds in attaining a kind of spiritual truth through the powerful grace of its architecture.

Galleries are graced with high ceilings—18 feet and 23 feet (5.5 meters and 7 meters) respectively on the fourth and fifth floors—and a sophisticated, carefully balanced blend of daylight and artificial light.

Meeting rooms, public gathering spaces, and retail stores—including the museum cafe and souvenir shop/bookstore shown here—surround the ground-floor atrium like shops around a piazza in an Italian town. The architect designed the furniture in the cafe; its glass walls connect the museum interior and the street.

The tiered, brick building is graced with a fantastic centerpiece—a striped granite-clad "giant eye," the cylindrical lantern tower at its center. The exterior brick is detailed with decorative patterning to soften the monolithic quality. This powerful, symmetrical structure has an ineffable, timeless quality to it that is reminiscent of a cathedral. It is also, ultimately, very simple to read, both inside and out, with galleries surrounding a central gathering space.

A LANDSCAPE OF FRAGMENTS

Charles Gwathmey's expansion and renovation of the Henry Art Gallery on Seattle's University of Washington campus is a clear, fully realized response to the complex demands of the site and program. Designed in the 1920s by Northwest architect Carl Gould, the original Henry was intended to be but one wing of a U-shaped arts complex with a matching music building to the south and a linking main hall forming a plaza between them. The plan was never realized, and the 10,000-square-foot (3,050-square-meter), Gothic Revival Henry stood alone for seventy years. During those years a pedestrian bridge, an underground parking garage, and several campus buildings went up near the Henry, making the realization of Gould's original vision impossible.

Fittingly, Gwathmey opposed building anything inspired by Gould on philosophical grounds: "Replication is not an option. The history of architecture has always been enriched through change, dialogue, additions to, interventions in, and renovations of existing buildings." The museum board asked that the addition expand the building from 10,000 square feet to 50,000 square feet (3,050 square meters to 15,250 square meters) and make the museum more accessible. The Gwathmey Siegel design team developed a plan to meet these needs while " . . . enriching the original, through a comprehensive . . . intervention." The strategy was to create "a landscape of fragments." While this describes the reality of the addition as seen from the outside, the plan in total is more complex.

All photos by Farshid Assassi/Assassi Productions

Overall views show how the multiple forms and volumes of the addition wrap around the east and south facades of the original Henry Art Gallery building at left in both photos. By placing most of the larger new galleries below the level of the original's main floor—the largest new space is located beneath the three elongated rectangular skylights—the architect kept open the gateway view into the University of Washington campus. Two paths of ingress—the bridge and the spiral stair with its glass-block lantern—frame the collage of fragments that define the addition above grade.

Gwathmey began by shifting the pedestrian bridge a few degrees south of its position perpendicular to the building, aligning it directly with the facade of a campus building also designed by Carl Gould and thus re-establishing the bridge as a gateway. This allowed the architects to excavate the Henry's south facade, in front of which a new exterior sculpture court fit neatly, below the shifted bridge. Spanning one side of the sculpture court, the bridge allows passersby to view the artworks. The bridge becomes "more than access," says Gwathmey. "It becomes a central part of the experience." The exposed lower facade also revealed expanses of cast stone that serve as the common element between old and new. Other materials in the addition include concrete, linen-finished stainless steel, and glass. The stone is the opaque, anchoring, "literal" material; the steel is reflective, ever-changing, the "elusive counterpoint."

Gwathmey designed the addition as a north-south linear structure paralleling the existing Henry on its east side, with a larger section extending to the south of the building below grade. At the southwest corner, a spiral staircase defines the building edge, and with the bridge frames the "fragmentary landscape" that rises out of the addition's rooftop/plaza: a trio of rectangles, another of pyramids, long, rectangular skylights in the main exhibition gallery roof, the glass-block lantern that floats atop the spiral stairs.

The architect moved the bridge spanning 15th Avenue away from its position in physical contact with the original Henry at left, freeing up the building and allowing the excavation of its lower level. A cafe was then installed, with doors opening onto the sculpture court. Now, pedestrians on the bridge are granted visual contact with the museum every time they pass. The circulation flow into the campus at rear is also more appropriately lined up on axis.

Glass cubes and pyramids allow light into the offices and galleries below, and shape a collage of intriguing architectural fragments on this primary pedestrian level. As is made clear in the juxtaposition of the old and new at rear, architect Charles Gwathmey believes in intervention, not replication. The new entrance to the complex is located in the new wing, at the end of the circulation path between the geometric skylights. The museum shop is adjacent to the reception desk.

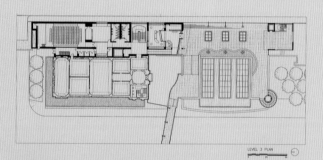

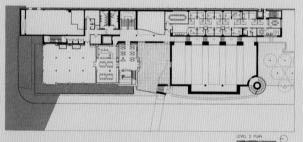

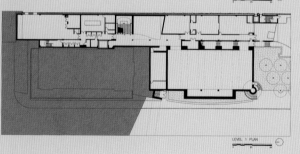

The meaning of the skylights remains elusive until one descends into the museum. The new entry foyer accesses the museum shop, education studio, and auditorium in the new wing along the north side of the original building. The renovated galleries in the original building, displaying the museum's permanent collection, are also on this upper level. A grand stair descends to the middle level, which contains the study center and the new cafe in the original building, along with the new sculpture court and skylit administrative offices. Another downward turn leads to the three new galleries: the East Gallery, the Media Gallery, and the grandest space of all, the double-height South Gallery, bathed in daylight from the skylights overhead.

This inversion of the expected order—descending to the largest, brightest, and most dramatic volume in the building—is the most compelling aspect of the design. To find this generously daylit and high-ceilinged space in the deepest reaches of the project is a revelation. Gwathmey's dictum that one should experience a museum as a sequence of varied spaces, a kind of unfolding and revealing of artworks with a continuous sense of surprise, has been executed brilliantly.

Three levels of floor plans show how the plaza and skylights on level 3 form roofs and allow light into levels 1 and 2. The original building is at bottom left, with only two levels.

Interior views show Gwathmey's spare, sculptural design at its best. When architectural gestures are few and subtle, each one takes on greater meaning and power. In the new East Gallery, a piece painted directly onto the wall stands out dramatically. Note the slight, sinuous curve of the line defining the edge of the gallery above and below. The South Gallery (opposite) is the largest volume in the complex, with daylight flooding in from rooftop skylights that lie on the plaza level above.

"PICTURE THIS"

A collaborative effort by architects, landscape architects, and an artist best known for working with aphoristic text, this project (phase one of a 167-acre (66.8-hectare) master plan entitled Imperfect Utopia: A Park for the New World) has transformed a drab, rural landscape adjacent to the North Carolina Museum of Art, a 1960s building by Edward Durrell Stone, into The Textualized Landscape. This multimedia site takes the notion of landscape art in an original new direction—one that rejects the received notions of outdoor art as it usually relates to art museums. "We were . . . working against the 'plaza plop' idea of art in the landscape," notes architect Laurie Hawkinson. "We wanted to bring people outside to explore this indigenous landscape."

All photos by Paul Warchol

Aerial views reveal the site's primary image, the words "picture this," made of letters of assorted materials. Each letter delivers its own message through materials, text, imagery, and other media. Several of the letters are actually parts of differing structures. The original 1960s museum building lies between the landscape installation and the parking lots.

On a functional level, The Textualized Landscape comprises performance stage, movie screen, and gathering spaces for assorted museum activities. Structures associated with these activities include The Big Roof, supported on a series of walking columns and a single truss over The Big Stage, a 40-foot by 60-foot (12.2-meter by 18.3-meter) concrete performance platform; the projection booth, a plywood box on a steel frame 12 feet (3.7 meters) above grade; The Big Screen, a 30-foot by 60-foot (9.1-meter by 18.3-meter) movie screen attached to the original museum building; an electrical back-building; the Amphitheater; and the Outdoor Cinema. These are the fundamental elements, archetypal, prosaic, and functional. The scale ranges from intimate to vast, designed to accommodate a single soul in a contemplative frame of mind, a crowd of several thousand to watch a movie on The Big Screen, and anything in between.

More significant are the simple words "picture this" in capitals large enough to be read from the sky. While the letters are all the same size, they are made in different materials, colors, textures, and depths, lending them sculptural qualities that infuse Kruger's typically flat, irony-laden aphorism with an architectural richness—enhanced by assorted messages culled from local history and contained within each letter. Some, like the second *T,* serve a structural purpose, housing bathrooms, storage, and a concession booth beneath an overlook. The second letter *I,* a sloped seating area for the Big Screen, is imprinted with the North Carolina state

The Big Roof over the amphitheater stage is intended to identify and focus the performance space in the landscape while providing shelter from rain and sun. Materials like painted plywood, corrugated metal, poured concrete, and chain-link fence are derived from the local building vernacular.

motto: To Be Rather Than To Seem, which takes on decidedly different interpretations in this context. Every letter has its meaning, as the site playfully yet profoundly examines the paradoxical relationships of text and texture, word and image, near and far, language, landscape, and structure. It makes a great place to watch movies or performances as well.

Materials form another level of meaning. Rather than build with traditional outdoor sculptural materials such as marble or bronze, the designers have built their odd assortment of structures, including letters, sheds, fences, and roofs, out of local vernacular materials like the corrugated tin commonly used to roof tobacco barns, along with aluminum, steel, cinder blocks, painted plywood, concrete, asphalt, and chain-link fencing. Quirky and compelling, the installation extends the museum into the outdoors, drawing attention to its regional and cultural context and infusing it with contemporary energy, while testing and dissolving the boundaries between art, architecture, and landscape design.

The Big Screen, a 30-foot by
60-foot (9.1-meter by 18.3-meter)
movie screen attached to the
original museum building, connects
the old structure with the new
landscape design.

Phoenix Art Museum
Phoenix, Arizona
Tod Williams, Billie Tsien and Associates, Architects

URBANISM IN THE DESERT

After Los Angeles, there is no city more symbolically western than Phoenix. The sweep of the migration west, having reached the coast, flowed back to the empty land passed over the first time—land that remains partially free of the cost, overcrowding, and regulation that can define contemporary life in Southern California. In spite of—or because of—this freedom, the creators of Phoenix have persisted in making architecture that is inoffensive yet unremarkable. But it does have contextual consistency; there is an attempt made to relate to the desert and to bond with the cultural history of the region.

In recent years the city has embarked on a course of self-improvement, and civic leaders decided to expand and improve the Phoenix Art Museum, located in a 1956 Alden Dow-designed building on Central Avenue. This 12-mile-long (19.2-kilometer-long) north-south thoroughfare serves as a primary urban artery, with clusters of high-rises strewn along both sides. One such cluster contains the Heard Museum of Native American Art, the Phoenix Public Library, and the Phoenix Art Museum and Theater Center.

All photos by Bill Timmerman

Views of the western Central Avenue facade. The two new wings slope toward the entry court at center. Banners, signage, exterior ramps, and interior ramp enclosures add color and layering to the north end of the facade. The

pre-cast aggregate panels that serve as the cladding on the primary volumes have a gray-green tinge, derived from imbedded quartz, that is suggestive of plants like paloverde trees and sagebrush.

The ramped central entry courtyard lies between the two new wings, which are linked by a gently sloping, metal-clad bridge. The metal is counterpointed by gray-green aggregate panels. The architects have selected a palette inspired by the desert but avoid the predictable shades of khaki. The entrance at night acts as a beacon, drawing passersby. Note the unusual locations of the apertures.

Onto this motorized landscape stepped New York architects Tod Williams, Billie Tsien and Associates. Constrained by the politics of public buildings and a tight budget, but above all challenged by the existing building and the elusive essence of Phoenix as an urban place, the architects took their cues from the existing structure and the traffic of Central Avenue. Paralleling the avenue, two new wings symmetrically flank a ramped central entry court. Their windowless precast panel facades pitch downward toward the center, signaling the entry and creating a linear dynamic most evident to those passing in cars. The scale and mass of the panels lend the structure a sense of gravity, of weight and density, "as if it had risen from the earth," according to the architects. Precast panels, made locally, were selected for financial reasons; and because their green tone, deriving from green quartzite, echoes the color of sagebrush and the paloverde trees of the desert.

Overhead, a metal-clad bridge linking the two wings spans the entry court, descending gradually, and asymmetrically, from left to right. The entry court leads into a lobby that links the existing and new buildings to the rear with the two new wings. The new right wing contains auditorium and gallery space, linked by stairs and ramps that are both circulatory and exhibition spaces and are animated with architectural vignettes. Consisting of overlooks, turns, landings, openings, and shifts in material, color, or texture, these vignettes infuse the interiors with urbane liveliness. The range of circulation zones reflects the architects' belief in the

Metal and glass are surprisingly appropriate desert materials, softened with reflected light and color. The glass wall faces east and will overlook the fiberglass sculpture pavilion when it is built.

importance of what is experienced by the pedestrian. This wing also houses the Great Hall, an elaborately detailed gathering place that will host openings. Across the central courtyard, the left wing has been designed as a space for changing exhibitions. Sheetrock walls and a changeable mechanical ceiling lend this loft-like space a more industrial feeling, enhanced with wooden floors and temporary dividing walls.

Screened by the mass of the new paneled wings, renovated and new structures to the rear contain permanent collection galleries, a cafe, a museum store, offices and functional spaces arrayed asymmetrically around a courtyard. The signifying form that will establish the institution as a star on the Phoenix cityscape is a translucent fiberglass sculpture pavilion that will be installed in the courtyard when funding becomes available. In a sense, it is unfair to evaluate this museum without it. Though possessed of a lively, brilliantly layered interior that is elegantly finished and organized, the structure's streetside exterior is muted without the pavilion; later, it will be transformed into a beacon to lend much-needed definition to a rather amorphous urban landscape.

Blurring the lines between circulation and exhibition space, the architects make the journey as important as the destination.

Everywhere in the interior, shifts in scale, texture, and color make movement through the space a kind of constant revelation.

The materials in the Great Hall— stone floors, wood ceiling systems—are more refined than in the other new wing, as this will be the site of openings, galas, and social events. Ramps and overlooks at far right are part of the circulation system linking the Great Hall with upper-level galleries and the auditorium on the lower level.

A blocky, sculpted stair linking the entry with temporary exhibition galleries on the upper level exemplifies the architects' use of shifting scales and materials to enrich the pedestrian experience.

GATHERING LIGHT

The Beyeler Foundation consists of three parts: the Berower Park lands, acquired by the foundation in 1976, the eighteenth-century Berower Villa housing the foundation's restaurant and offices, and the new museum building, designed by Renzo Piano to house the 160 works of art that comprise the Beyeler collection.

The narrow museum building, which opened in 1997, occupies a site between a busy connecting road and a protected agricultural and natural area. Reflecting and echoing the presence of old walls that once enclosed the site, the essence of the low-rise structure is simple: four 394-feet-long (120-meter-long) load-bearing walls lie parallel, 23 feet (7 meters) apart. In addition to dividing the interior into a series of precisely scaled galleries, these walls help support a glass roof. On the side facing the road, a windowless fifth wall encloses the section of the building that contains the bookshop, coatrooms, and other nongallery spaces. Opposite it, a sixth, longitudinal wall shelters a winter garden with a view to the tree-filled park land outside, a place for visitors to relax. By putting the service and reception areas along these east and west facades, the architects maintain the heart of the building as display space, assuring that "nothing disturbs the visual calm to which the museum aspires," notes Piano.

The exterior containing walls are constructed of roughly finished red porphyry imported from Patagonia. At the ends of the long, low structure, glass walls permit vistas into adjacent gardens, enriching the flow of internal light and enhancing the interplay of interior and exterior, of nature and structure. Accessed via stairs in the winter garden, the basement level houses a 1,025-square-foot (311-square-meter) gallery designated for temporary exhibitions.

All photos by Michel Denancé

Seen from the adjacent park and agricultural lands, the long, low museum building blends gently into the surrounding greenery. The roof is glass and steel, the exterior walls porphyry. On this side, facing the park, glass walls permit views of the outdoors and lend the structure a transparent quality.

Bathed in natural light streaming in through the glass roof 26 feet (8 meters) above the floor, the galleries are luminous, inviting spaces. Each gallery is scaled at 23 feet by 36 feet (7 by 11 meters), or fractions or multiples thereof, and the repetition, counterpointed by the striking, individualistic qualities of the art on display, lends a kind of geometrically induced serenity to the space.

The roof is made of steel and glass, and covers 43,055 square feet (4,000 square meters), but it rests delicately, almost weightlessly atop the structure.

Responding to client Ernst Beyeler's request for a space infused with "luxury, calm, and sensuality," the Building Workshop developed an original roof system made entirely of glass and steel. Resting lightly on the internal walls and supports tucked into greenery around the building, the 43,055 square feet (4,000 square meters) of glass roof float 26 feet (8 meters) above the floor. This permits daylight to flow into the galleries in a natural state, channeling and modulating it, responding sensitively to the changes wrought by weather and time.

The galleries are arranged in a nonlinear fashion to allow visitors to find their way easily without feeling the pressure of a defined circulation path.

Enhanced by artificial light when daylight is insufficient, the galleries are spare, peaceful spaces. The serenity is produced in part by the absence of distracting ornamentation or details as is evident in the seamless joining of walls to ceiling and the light-colored French oak flooring. It is furthered by the relaxing counterpoint of repetition and variety—each gallery is precisely 23 feet by 36 feet (7 by 11 meters) or a multiple of that measure, yet each contains striking, original, and very different works of art. Most importantly, the tranquil ambiance results from the quality of the interior light. As Piano notes, "Everything in this project contributes to harnessing light in the service of art."

Site Section

Site section and site plan lend a sense of scale and illustrate how lightly the building rests in and on the landscape.

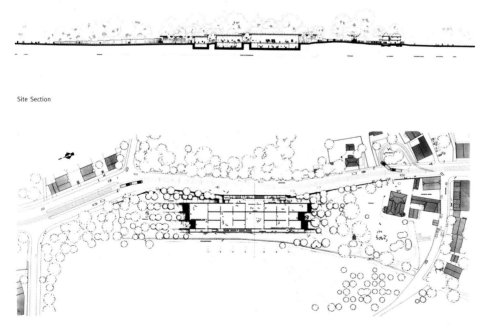

Site Plan

Ponds and plantings create a transitional zone between the museum and the surrounding park lands. Imported from Patagonia, the mottled, roughly textured porphyry stone utilized in the walls provides a quiet, appealing contrast with the greenery and the finely finished structural elements.

A photograph with an overlay (above) and the site plan (opposite) show how the museum building occupies a long, narrow site tucked in between a busy road and open agricultural lands.

NEOCLASSICAL SIMPLICITY

The Thyssen-Bornemisza Museum contains a collection of more than 800 masterworks, ranging from medieval to contemporary, from the private collection of the German industrialist Baron Thyssen-Bornemisza, whose gift of these works to the nation of Spain hinged on establishing an appropriate museum to display them. Villahermosa Palace, a handsome neoclassical building located near the Prado in Madrid, best met this requirement. The three-story palace had undergone a number of renovations in the two hundred years since being constructed, rendering the interiors a chaotic jumble.

Spanish architect Jose Rafael Moneo was selected to transform chaotic palace into ordered museum. Moneo, an admirer of tradition and a maker of spare, unadorned structures, elected to leave the austere exterior facades of the building alone, concentrating his efforts on a complete reorganization of the interiors and a new roof.

He began by establishing a new, north-south axis relating to the north entrance, where an enclosed garden creates a gentle transitional zone between busy street and quiet museum. Within the building, on the ground floor and two upper floors Moneo placed galleries around the perimeters, dividing the spaces according to the rhythm established by the existing window grid. The palette is white, off-white, and, predominantly, rosy pink.

At the center of the building on ground level, Moneo created a large, quiet volume, traditionally called a *zaguan,* a still, contemplative zone. Though it is open to a high, illuminated ceiling, the long, narrow space is not surrounded by easily accessible galleries, nor does it contain the main staircase. The room's walls are finished in pink plaster and hung with a few paintings and tapestries. The room is also decorated with potted plants (installed over the objections of the architect). From the entry, visitors pass directly into this space, which is intended to move visitors into a quieter frame of mind for studying the art.

The entry lobby has marble floors in a pattern of squares, diamonds, and triangles. Beyond the entry dividers and control desk, visitors enter the zaguan, the overscale space at the heart of the museum. Unlike an atrium or courtyard, this is a place not of movement but of stillness and contemplation; thus there are no openings to galleries and few artworks. At foreground left, a portal provides access to the contemporary gallery area and is used by visitors exiting the upper levels.

Visitors enter the museum through the quiet transition space provided by a garden and patio adjacent to the north facade of the late eighteenth-century building. The architect changed little on the handsome, unadorned exterior facades.

All photos by José Latova Fernández-Luna

The warm pink, centrally located zaguan extends upwards to the level of the ceilings, with myriad openings on the second floor allowing views into this tranquil volume. Access is limited to the museum entry seen at rear (top), and the rectangular opening seen at the far end of the pink wall (left). The portraits at lower right feature the museum's patron, Baron Thyssen-Bornemisza, and his wife (left).

The upstairs galleries are then accessed via a staircase and elevators separated from the *zaguan* by a thick wall and reached through a rectangular portal. The artworks are hung chronologically, encouraging visitors to begin with Renaissance works on the top floor, circling the central void on each floor as they descend. On the top floor, spacious galleries are accessed off a wide promenade along the eastern or main facade paralleling Paseo del Prado. This promenade, like many of the spaces on the gallery levels, serves as both circulation pathway and gallery. Illumination on the top floor is provided by a row of light-admitting boxes installed on the roof above pyramid-shaped ceilings, while a more traditional enfilade arrangement allows second floor galleries access to natural light from existing windows. On the ground floor, most perimeter galleries are hidden behind the high walls of the *zaguan* and display works of twentieth-century and experimental vintage. A basement-level gallery reached by separate stairs off the entry complements the permanent collections upstairs with temporary exhibitions, a lecture hall, and a cafe.

After exiting the galleries, visitors may shop in the museum store or linger in the garden. On viewing the entry facade from the garden, it becomes clear that in shaping this museum of paintings and sculptures, Moneo has created twentieth-century interiors that quietly harmonize with eighteenth-century exteriors.

Top floor display areas are bathed in light from a row of light boxes installed on the roof.

Plans show the galleries arranged around the central open area, or zaguan, which is roofed over at the top floor level. On the ground floor, the museum is accessed off the garden, with its rows of plantings and elegant stone patio. The basement level contains rest rooms and back-of-house facilities as well as a cafe, lecture hall, and temporary exhibition space.

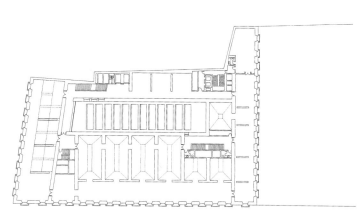

Second-Floor Plan

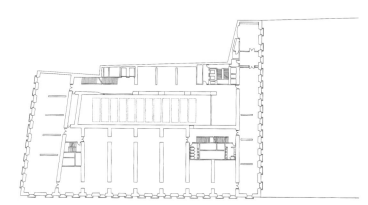

First-Floor Plan

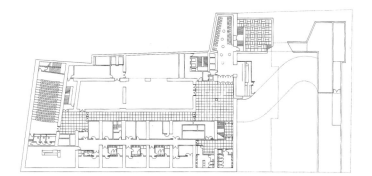

Basement-Level Plan

Pink-hued galleries are arranged along circulation axes that also serve as display space, with perpendicular walls of differing scales arranged to vary the shapes and sizes of galleries. Even a quick glance at the works reveals that the Thyssen-Bornemisza collection is remarkable in its range and depth.

L.A. ACROPOLIS

Executed in the classically graceful yet modern style that has made Richard Meier one of the most successful museum architects of the late twentieth century, the Getty Center is the most ambitious museum project in the modern world. A monumental, billion-dollar acropolis set on a hilltop above a freeway on the west side of Los Angeles, the Getty will remain unrivaled in terms of sheer scale and grandeur for decades to come.

View looking south over the complex, sited on a hill in West Los Angeles. The multistructure Getty Museum is at top, accessed from the circular rotunda. At far right is positioned the circular Research Institute for the History of Art and the Humanities. At bottom lies the restaurant/cafe. To the left of the access road are the auditorium, and the north and east buildings.

Beyond finance and scale, how will the buildings fare as objects and cultural elements in the sub/urban fabric of Los Angeles? Whether the institution's isolated position on a 110-acre (44-hectare) hilltop site in L.A.'s pricey West Side generates a kind of aloof elitism that diminishes its impact as a cultural center remains to be seen. But given an enormous endowment and the scale of the complex, there is no doubt that as scholarly sanctuary and aesthetic cathedral, the Getty Center has the potential to rank among the most significant cultural institutions in the world.

The complexities of planning an institution of this size are staggering; thus it is no surprise that when the Getty Center was completed at the end of 1997, about eight years had passed since the first soil was turned on the parking structure that lies 3/4 of a mile (1.2 kilometers) from the museum. In the years since, a cluster of low-rise buildings have been constructed within a 5-acre (2-hectare) space on the 24-acre (9.6-hectare) campus; they are densely confined to minimize the effects on the landscape. Shaped to the contours of the two ridges that provide the hilltop site, along with the five linked structures that form the J. Paul Getty Museum, six other buildings house the Getty Research Institute for the History of Art and the Humanities, the Getty Conservation Institute, The Getty Education Institute for the Arts, the Getty Grant Program, the Getty Trust offices, an auditorium, and a restaurant/cafe. The remaining 19 acres (7.6 hectares) will be devoted to landscaped outdoor space, including a central garden designed by California artist Robert Irwin. To further curtail intrusions on the landscape, museum-goers will be delivered from the underground parking area to the museum complex by electric tram. The buildings devoted to non-museum activities are clad in Meier's signature matte-finished aluminum panels and clear glazing, but the museum buildings are covered primarily in Italian travertine marble.

All photos by Tom Bonner (except as noted)

The entry pavilion to the
J. Paul Getty Museum is clad in
matte white metal panels; the
gallery buildings, arrayed around
a central garden behind the
entry, are finished in imported
travertine marble.

Travertine marble blocks and aluminum panels are the primary exterior finish materials at the Getty Museum, with the metal panels also utilized as cladding on the Getty Center's other buildings.

Photo by Alex Vertikoff

Housing the Getty's permanent collection, the 360,000-square-foot (32,400-square-meter) museum is the focal point of the complex. The museum is organized into smaller buildings, accessed from a cylindrical entry lobby providing views through a courtyard to the galleries. The gallery buildings are linked by bridges, passages, and balconies designed to enhance the interplay of interior and exterior—and to allow visitors spectacular views of the outside world. The galleries are arrayed sequentially, reflecting both the time period and the medium, and providing a logical progression around the courtyard. Within each structure, paintings occupy the upper level to take advantage of natural light, while more light-sensitive works are sheltered below. The arrangement offers visitors a chance to experience the museum chronologically within one medium,

A detail of the museum courtyard, enclosed by marble-and-glass walls.

Photo by Alex Vertikoff

passing from building to building on the same level, or to explore all the media of a given time period within one structure.

An interior designer commissioned after the architecture had been planned has created a series of interior galleries that utilize period elements to more sympathetically display the museum's historic holdings; yet this period styling runs counter to the intention of the architecture. How this interplay of contemporary architecture and period-influenced interior design will work in the long run is an open question—one of many still to be answered. Nevertheless, Meier's vastly ambitious architectural plan for this equally ambitious institution is now a fait accompli. The Getty will serve as one of the premier cultural centers in the world for many years.

The buildings and circulation paths have been designed to
maximize accessibility to the panoramic views of Los Angeles and
the rich daylight of Southern California.

A westerly view from the East
Building, looking towards the ramp
leading from the arrival plaza to the
museum offices. The clean, spare
detailing, seen here in the railings,
along with glass and matte metal,
are counterpointed by the organic
richness of rough-cut stone.

Photo by Alex Vertikoff

Assorted galleries in the North and West Pavilions display paintings from nineteenth-century Europe (above), and the Renaissance (right). The warmly painted walls and other details are characteristic of the period galleries, where the interior designers have created backdrops that are more responsive to the contents rather than the architecture of the buildings.

The Decorative Arts Galleries
are finished with colors and
textures that reflect their holdings.
Shown here is the Gallery of
French Decorative Arts from
1750 to 1760.

A Renaissance Bronze Sculpture
Gallery in the North Pavilion of
the museum features Mercury,
from 1570 to 1580, by Johan
Gregor van der Schardt.

The Gallery of French Decorative Arts features tapestries from 1690 to 1705 from a series called L'Histoire de L'Empereur de la Chine. *Some feel that the museum's* interior finishes, with their period details designed to reflect contents, run counter to the more contemporary qualities of the architecture.

SPECIALIZED
art museums

WARHOL'S POP PALACE

The building's original exterior facade is elaborately detailed terra-cotta. This, along with the blue, tapering plaster walls of the entry passage, lend dramatic punch to the Warhol self-portrait on the inner wall.

To those who witnessed the surprisingly long-lived career of the sadly short-lived Andy Warhol, the very existence of a museum dedicated to his work is somewhat ironic, but not because his art isn't significant. Serious critics place him close to the top among influential artists of the latter half of the twentieth century. The issue is not quality but ephemerality. Warhol was inspired by the buzz and flash of pop culture, and its artifacts are, by definition, throwaway. Putting these food boxes, soup cans, and silver celebrity portraits in the hallowed halls of a museum seems completely paradoxical.

This leads to another irony: Warhol was a creature of New York, and yet his museum is in Pittsburgh, his birthplace, hardly the setting for any important Warhol events, and thus something of an odd choice for a museum housing the most extensive collection of his work. It includes 900 pieces of art and 608 boxes ("time capsules") crammed with correspondence, party invitations, cookie jars, all the detritus of one of the great party animals of the twentieth century who was also an obsessive shopper and pack rat. Every night Warhol would go through his day's accumulated stuff and drop whatever he deemed interesting in a cardboard box at his bedside. When the box was full, he'd seal and date it, then start another one. Thus the 608 boxes.

Ground floor volumes flanking the entry include an information room to the left of the oval-shaped galvanized-steel ticket booth. The museum store flanks the entry on the other side. Ochre walls in these areas distinguish them from the white-walled gallery spaces. The information plaques are positioned in the same place on each floor to help with orientation.

All photos by Paul Rocheleau

In addition to replacing the cornice and restoring the terra-cotta facade of the circa-1911 Pittsburgh building that houses the museum, the architect designed the 50-foot by 50-foot (15.2-meter by 15.2-meter) annex at right. The annex contains offices, elevators, a theater, archival storage rooms, and mechanical equipment.

Auxiliary spaces include the archive/research area and a 110-seat auditorium furnished with re-upholstered chairs from a New York theater originally designed by Marcel Breuer. In the archive room, museum-goers can watch researchers go through Warhol's 608 "time capsules" behind the glass walls at right.

The luminous glow around Gluckman's new stairwell is intended to attract people. The idea is to ascend via elevator to the top floor, then descend one floor at a time by the stairs.

The museum, a joint venture of the Andy Warhol Foundation, the Dia Center for the Arts, and the Carnegie Institute, has been designed by New York architect Richard Gluckman. The seven-story former Frick and Lindsay building that houses the museum was constructed in 1911. Gluckman restored the terra-cotta exterior, replaced the crumbling cornice, and replaced a 1918 addition with a 50-foot by 50-foot (15.2-meter by 15.2-meter) annex containing staff offices, a theater, archival storage, elevators, and mechanical equipment.

Gluckman's understated interiors provide an appropriately subtle backdrop for the intense colors and repetitive, over-scale Warhol artworks. However, there is more to this project than organizing and lighting walls. The building has low ceilings, and the architect was unable to distribute temperature-control systems horizontally behind dropped ceilings. Instead, he installed a multipurpose box within a box, floating clean new walls four feet inside the building's original shell, then distributing the HVAC systems and light wells vertically behind the new walls.

The sense of entering a building within a building is most evident at street level. Inside the glass entry doors, walls of blue plaster and a silver-leaf ceiling taper inward, creating a funnel-like space of converging planes that opens into a gallery, dominated by a wild-haired Warhol self-portrait. Dramatically visible from the street, this sets the tone for the whole museum.

Also on street level are the essential accessories of the modern museum: ticket-taking, information, coat check, and retail. Throughout the building, Gluckman has delineated orientation and circulation space with ochre walls, while the walls utilized to hang art are white. The architect shaped a variety of spaces to accommodate the different Warhol modes of presentation; for example, he placed cinematic, repetitive pieces like the Shadow series and the silver Elvises on long, horizontal walls, with the works extending beyond the frame of the building. For the *Skulls* series, Gluckman removed a column to create a large, empty cube in the heart of the building. As is evident throughout, Gluckman has mined the two-dimensional Warhol iconography for three-dimensional inspiration, making spaces that clarify the power of Warhol's work, with its unsettling familiarity.

For repetitive, filmstrip-inspired works like Seventeen Elvises and Shadows, Gluckman created rooms that extend the works imaginatively beyond the walls. Note the new, tapered plaster finish on existing columns and the translucent light monitors in the ceiling. For the Skulls piece, Gluckman created a high, windowless cube at the heart of the museum.

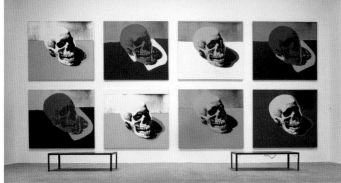

THE ARTIST AND THE ARCHITECT

Over the last several decades, few South Koreans have been recognized internationally for their achievements. Among them are the late painter Kim Whanki and the Boston-based architect Kyu Sung Woo; so it is fitting that Kyu Sung Woo design the Whanki Museum, dedicated to the preservation and display of Kim Whanki's work.

Tucked into the Buam Dong Valley on the northern edge of Seoul, the museum synthesizes architectural traditions from East and West, forging a modern container for the contemporary paintings of Kim Whanki. Chosen for its accessibility and proximity to mountain landscapes, the Buam Dong Valley is populated with residences and shops linked by narrow, winding streets. The walled compound is a Korean tradition, a design response to rough terrain; the Whanki Museum honors that tradition within its gated wall. Situated along the east-west axis of the valley, the museum is low-rise and relatively small to blend in with its neighbors.

Given the steep grades, the architect planned two separate structures: the museum and the annex, a two-story rectangular structure housing shops, a cafe, and temporary exhibition space below the main building. The concrete brick annex, like the wall surrounding the compound, contrasts with the richer tones of the granite cladding and the lead-coated copper roofs of the main building. In conjunction with the gated entrance and the compound's terraced landscaping, the annex establishes an appealing arrival sequence.

The museum is sited in a narrow valley in an urban residential area on the north side of Seoul. Like most of the residences in the area, the museum compound is contained within a wall with a gate providing entry at the lower end of the sloping site. The wall and
annex are finished in concrete blocks, while the museum building is clad in granite blocks. The main building is partially buried in the ground to allow higher-ceilinged galleries without violating the low-rise character of the neighborhood.

The main building can be likened to a traditional Korean palace or a village, in that there are distinct pieces united by a central courtyard. This separation of elements is also a way of adapting to the hilly site, as sections of the building step up along the slope. By embedding the structure into a basin set deeply in the hillside, the architect was able to create high-ceilinged galleries to display Whanki's larger canvases without violating low-rise neighborhood harmony.

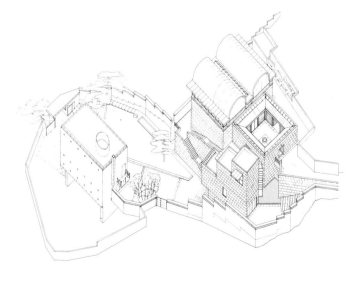

Axonometric illustrates the sharp contrast between the simplicity of the rectangular annex and the complex main museum building—and also how the highly irregular shape of the site is enclosed within a defining wall. Many Korean houses are thus enclosed, for it is a logical design response to the difficulties inherent in building and defining spatial relationships on rough, hilly terrain. The importance of the courtyard as a central, unifying element is clear. The steel frame of the museum building is set in a concrete basin carved into the mountain.

All photos by Timothy Hursley

Accessed via stairs from the central hall, the spacious, double-vaulted gallery that crowns the entire structure houses a permanent collection of Whanki paintings. The opening framed by the two vaults offers a dramatic perspective on the craggy peaks of In Wang Mountain.

Accessed from a high, narrow hall, the heart of the museum is a 26-foot (7.9-meter) cube, a double-walled space capped with an exterior court-yard. The inner cube of this central hall is surrounded with spiraling stairs positioned between the two layers of wall. The stairs are visible through the upper reaches of the inner cube, and from them the buildings' intri-cate circulation patterns, or ribbons, are generated. These ribbons are not planned for ease of movement but are experiential, offering the museum-goer an array of vistas from terraces, courts, stairs, and passages linking the building's several levels as well as the landscaped surroundings. The play of inward and outward, courtyard and view, reflects what the archi-tect calls "the traditional [Korean] concept of inwardly focused space coex-isting with a newly acquired sense of outwardness." The interior spaces, especially the large central gallery, are lent the warmth of the outside world through the courtyard's glass block walls, oculus, and skylights, which flood the white-walled interiors with daylight.

Proximate to and above the central hall is the double-vaulted gallery, a spacious volume with vaults flanking a view of In Wang Mountain. The museum's permanent collection of Whanki paintings are displayed here, illuminated by artificial light and daylight reflecting from the high vaults. This gallery opens into the courtyard that sits atop the central hall. Exposed to the sky yet enclosed on four sides with glass-block walls under slanted tin roofs, this courtyard is empty but for the light well at its center. The graceful exteriors of the symmetrical vaults loom overhead, curving mountain shapes echoed by views of the real mountains. The for-mal and geometric echoes and counterpoints are precise—vault and mountain, glass and stone, circle and square, ground and sky. They lend an almost metaphysical quality to this empty, ordered space, contrasting powerfully with the landscape and the lyrical play of light, form, and art that distinguishes the museum interiors.

Adjacent to the double-vaulted gallery and capping the central hall, this rooftop courtyard ringed by glass-block walls is an austerely simple outdoor room that serves during the day as a light gatherer for the galleries below. The space is almost metaphysically serene, and offers a dramatic geometric counterpoint to the rugged hills surrounding the compound.

View from inside the entry gate at the lower end of the site. The concrete-brick clad annex is at immediate right, with the museum proper at left up the hill. The museum building entrance is at the lowest level in the stepped volume at center. The terraced landscapes provide natural contrast to the geometric ordering of the buildings.

These perspectives (below) taken from the stairs inserted between two layers of wall surrounding the central hall, and straight up from the hall itself, show how the skylights and glass-block walls of the courtyard on the roof flood the interior with light that shifts in color at different times of day.

Assorted views of the building exterior illustrate the myriad perspectives and spatial experiences generated by the architecture, particularly the meandering circulation paths that originate in the stairs surrounding the central hall. Varied granite masonry finishes offer subtle color shifts, and contrast with the lead roofing, the concrete brick of the compound's enclosing walls, and the hilly terrain and sky.

Shiga Kogen Roman Art Museum
Nagano, Japan
Kisho Kurokawa Architect & Associates

ELEMENTS OF LUMINOUS DARKNESS

This elegant small museum designed by the Japanese architect Kisho Kurokawa is situated at the base of the Kanbayashi Ski Run in the Shiga Kogen Ski Resort, host to the Nagano Olympics in 1998. The client, the town of Yamanouchi, was the birthplace of the Chinese-style painter Katei Kodama, and thus the museum will house about seventy of his works, along with artifacts from the Edo, Meiji, and Taisho eras. The museum's other primary collection—the collection that gives the institution its name—is one of ancient Roman and iridescent glass. The glass collection will be displayed in elegantly sculptural conical-glass cases designed for the project by the architect.

The museum comprises two structures linked by an enclosed connecting corridor with a transparent glass wall and a double door on one side. At one end of this connector, the primary volume is a two-story, reinforced concrete structure shaped into a kind of fragmentary ellipse wrapped around an inner oval. The incomplete ellipse, subtly evoking a natural landscape that has been eroded by water or wind, leaves one end of the inner oval volume exposed, and here, between angular walls formed by the truncated ellipse, the architect has located the building's main entrance. An angled ramp accesses the entrance, signaled with a shade pavilion and a vertical, gridded glass section of wall that wraps over the

All photos by Tomio Ohashi

Day and night views of the museum sited at the base of a ski mountain show the two distinct forms—the fragmentary ellipse of the museum proper, at left, and the glass cone housing the shop and

cafe, right. At night, the luminous glass cone acts as a lantern, signaling the presence of the museum. A connecting passage is transparent on one side.

edge of the building to extend onto the roof plane as a skylight. Crowned with a roof that has been gently sloped to prevent snow accumulation, the cast-concrete exterior is decorated with dozens of triangular pieces of polished metal, randomly situated and flush with its surface; they absorb and reflect light, creating a shifting dynamic that is subtly enhanced by the still, reflective surface of the stream that winds around the building, relating further with the natural surroundings.

From the entrance lobby, a skylit, concrete-finished passage leads into the dark, sepulchral interior volume of the central exhibition gallery, surrounded on the first floor by offices and other auxiliary space. A staircase provides access to the second-level exhibition galleries that wrap mezzanine-like around the open void at center. High over this space, the building's most startling element, an ovoid central section of the wooden ceiling, serenely floats, its inner form a ship-like shape separated from the outer section by the outline of a light cove; the outer section is then surrounded

by darkness. The effect is not unlike looking into the hull of an ancient ship—a Roman galley? The presence of this softly glowing wooden ceiling, patterned with sunken light fixtures and bound together with crossing beams, exposed rods, brackets, and other metallic elements, provides a powerful counterpoint to the cool geometry of the moody interior.

The other visual drama in the exhibition space is provided by the architect's glass display cones. Illuminated by light fixtures built into each one, they sit in rows in the cool darkness, marvelous things in and of themselves—the most artful of containers for artworks.

The cone is a favorite Kurokawa form, and he has used it in elements both large and small in this project. Along with the display cases, the architect has created a tall, glass, cone-shaped building to house the museum shop and cafe. Located at the other end of the connector from the main body of the museum, it acts as a light, gravity-defying counterpoint to the more solidly grounded main building. Illuminated at night, it also serves as a lantern, signaling the museum's presence. Linked by the connecting corridor, together they comprise a unique, architecturally sophisticated small museum. The museum's subtly luminous interiors are perfectly suited for the quiet pleasures to be had in experiencing the objects on display.

Stairs linking the first and second levels illustrate the architect's use of clean, crisply executed forms and finishes.

*High overhead, a skylight traces
the course of the corridor that links
the entry lobby with the main
ground-floor exhibition gallery.*

The architect designed the elegant, elongated cones that serve as display cases in the main exhibition gallery. With light fixtures built in, the cones are self-contained; the room can be left in semidarkness to heighten the impact of the illuminated objects. Ambient light is provided by fixtures sunk into the wooden ceiling and by the light cove between the ceiling's inner and outer sections.

These images demonstrate the startling beauty of a wooden ceiling floating like a ship across the darkness of the main exhibition gallery ceiling. A deep light cove separates the inner and outer sections. The combination of long planks, heavy crossbeams, and metal bracings enhances the ship-like quality established by the shape. The light from the cove makes another kind of art on the walls.

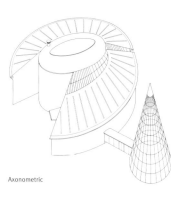

Axonometric shows the two distinct buildings and their connecting passage. The central oval form houses the double-height main exhibition gallery, with two levels of offices and gallery space wrapping around it. The museum shop and cafe are in the cone, which is clad in transparent glass.

Axonometric

Second-Floor Plan

First-Floor Plan

The view from the second-level lends a better sense of the scale and structure of the wooden ceiling (opposite). The objects on display are snuffboxes.

AN AFRICAN JOURNEY IN SOHO

The Museum for African Art is located in the storefront and basement level of an 1859 building in New York City's SoHo District. Visitors enter through a stand of tubular-copper trees.

Maya Lin's design for The Museum for African Art in New York City's SoHo District resembles her Vietnam Memorial Wall in Washington, D.C. in that she does the unexpected. The Vietnam Memorial Wall, of course, has turned out to be among the most powerful war memorials ever built. While the fate of The Museum for African Art likely will not be quite so dramatic, it represents another quietly imaginative, remarkable effort by Lin—unique primarily in that the design does not embrace overly adorned Africana in its architectural motifs; nor does it go the opposite way and utilize the contemporary style of stark white display space to avoid establishing any cultural context whatsoever. Instead, Lin has found middle ground, making a place that will gently introduce visitors to and educate them about the complexities of African art.

The museum is housed in a renovated storefront and basement space in an historic 1859 SoHo building and includes galleries for exhibitions on contemporary and historic themes, an events room for dance, video, music, or other performances, a museum store, and offices for a staff of sixteen. The low-cost design was created in collaboration with museum director Susan Vogel, her curatorial staff, and architect David Hotson.

The interior is a flowing blend of open spaces and modern forms integrated with African materials and colors that effectively bring the works into the foreground without posing them too self-consciously or surrounding them with culturally loaded African symbols. The circulation path meanders from foreground darkness toward the brilliant glow at the back of the space where a bright-yellow spiral stair links the main floor with the basement level. Along the way, visitors experience the museum store and the quiet, richly hued exhibition areas, where the works are arrayed in a continuous and changing display that reflects the everyday presence of art in African life. There is no way to re-create the animation and energy of the village life, performance, and ritual within which these objects normally exist, but the seemingly organic quality of the design does avoid completely decontextualizing them. There is a risk in not posing these exotic objects in stark white surroundings, for to some extent this meandering plan and the earthier colors tend to lessen the impact of individual objects. However, as an educational and aesthetic journey into African history and culture, without condescension or patronization, this approach is more authentic and, ultimately, more successful.

All photos by Paul Warchol

The reception desk, made of maple plywood and steel from a freehand drawing by Maya Lin, lies behind the museum shop on the ground floor. Artifacts are displayed on paneled shelving made of waxed masonite. Muted colors provide a more organic, natural ambience, and the objects are arrayed in an informal fashion to suggest the way art objects are integrated into the everyday life of African peoples.

In the Events Room, the benches were made from the floor joists of the original structure. The walls are covered in tie-dyed damask from the Ivory Coast.

A dance platform from Zaire rests on a floor that has been stained a deep greenish blue to suggest water. Sculptural objects are moved out from the wall and lit from above to emphasize their three-dimensional qualities.

The spiraling staircase is painted in five different shades of yellow, progressing from lighter to darker to emphasize the outward motion of the spiral. Irregular cutouts frame glimpses of gallery exhibits.

A SUCCESSFUL REBIRTH

The recent changes at Seattle's Frye Museum are as much a revelation as a renovation and expansion. This small, privately run institution, housing a collection of primarily nineteenth-century German paintings that once belonged to Seattle meatpacking magnate Charles Frye and his wife Emma, has been utterly transformed. The accomplishment is impressive because lead architect Rick Sundberg, FAIA, and his Olson Sundberg design team were limited by a tight budget and the terms of the museum endowment written into Frye's will. The will requires the Fryes' personal collection remain intact and that it be displayed in natural light, in no less than three 30-foot by 60-foot (9.1-meter by 18.3-meter) galleries, in a museum free to the public. The museum also may only display artworks in the same stylistic vein as the Fryes' original collection—figurative or representational.

The original Frye opened in 1952, twelve years after Frye's death, on First Hill behind downtown Seattle. The building was designed by modernist architect Paul Thiry in the unadorned International style of the time, which now seems inappropriate for a collection of figurative European paintings

Interior photos by Robert Pisano
Exterior photos by Strode Eckert Photographics

A new cafe, reflecting pool, and interior courtyard provide the museum with an enhanced street presence and attractive new amenities. The requirement for a handicapped ramp, right, inspired the long arcade with a reflecting pool alongside. The domed tower is a new vertical element that signals the museum's location.

New bronze doors open into the cylindrical foyer crowned with a steel dome floating overhead. The off-centered oculus indicates the location of the information booth. Slots admit light and views in and out and offer intriguing vignettes of the galleries.

of nineteenth and early twentieth-century vintage. Over the decades, three other architects added on to the building. By 1995, First Hill was locally known as Pill Hill, and the Frye was a modernist box burdened with clashing additions; the museum and its collection were old before their time.

Without breaking any of Frye's provisions, Sundberg remade the building, achieving an architectural harmony that eluded his predecessors and giving the institution new life. First, the existing galleries were revitalized with light and color. The architects raised the ceilings to bring in more daylight from existing monitors, installed wood floors, and painted the walls in varying shades of eggplant. By complementing the artworks rather than contrasting with them, these warm colors work better than white as a backdrop for the dark undertones of nineteenth-century paintings.

The building as a whole has been reborn as well through carefully considered expansion along the museum's two public street facades. Coupled with the renovations in the existing spaces, the additions highlight the better qualities of the building by establishing a unified sensibility. A grand, new arcade expands the structure into closer contact with the street, as a handicapped ramp, paralleling the sidewalk, gradually rises alongside a new reflecting pool and waterfall to meet the stairs at the building's entrance. After passing through an outer vestibule and elegantly detailed bronze doors, visitors will find the museum's great new space, the cylindrical entry lobby, crowned with a steel dome that floats overhead, glowing with filtered light from an off-centered oculus. The dome's exterior lends the museum a powerful new street presence; the interior offers a dramatic yet serene transitional space, allowing the eye time to adjust before entering the galleries, where art conservation requires lower levels of light.

From this domed entry lobby at the corner of the building, all the renovated galleries are easily accessible, as are the new facilities, including a museum cafe with outdoor dining, a retail store, a 142-seat auditorium, and an 8,000-square-foot (720-square-meter), two-story educational wing, complete with loft-style studios for painting and ceramics. The art-storage and conservation areas have been renovated, while temperature, humidity, light control, and other systems have been modernized.

This very personal museum, that long operated as a kind of public/private salon for the dwindling number of people interested in the conservative artworks it displayed, has been readied to face the twenty-first century without giving up a shred of its dignity and steadfastly remaining free to the public. With all the outreach, educational, and market-savvy accoutrements required for today's museum, the Frye is firmly established as an attractive, permanent home for its lovely, venerable collection. Without resorting to postmodern tricks, Olson Sundberg has crafted a fine, new home for the Frye's premodern tenants.

The entry foyer as seen from the interior, with the new retail store visible at the center, rear. The information booth in the entry foyer is visible at the end of the long circulation axis, with galleries for touring exhibitions at left (above). The works of living master Odd Nerdrum on display in this exhibit demonstrate the possibilities for powerful, psychologically intense imagery within the parameters of the figurative work that is the museum's special focus.

Renovations of existing spaces included raising the ceilings to enhance the flow of natural light into the galleries, putting in new floors, and painting galleries different shades of gray and eggplant to bring out the rich undertones of the nineteenth and early twentieth-century artworks in the Frye's permanent collections.

A new, dome-topped, cylindrical
lobby and a long arcade over the
handicapped ramp paralleling
the sidewalk lend the museum
a much-needed street presence in
a neighborhood containing
numerous high and medium-rise
health-care facilities.

These views show the new handicapped ramp/arcade, with its alternating single and double arches establishing a compelling rhythm alongside the reflecting pool that lies between the arcade and the museum proper. The cafe lies at one end of the arcade axis, the outer vestibule at the other. Raw, natural, and undecorated materials—stone, water, steel, and concrete—provide a surprising variety of subtle colors and textures.

OTHER
history, science, and special collections museums

UNPREDICTABLE GEOMETRY

As a practicing Buddhist and one of the prime movers behind the avant-garde Japanese architectural movement known as *metabolism,* the Japanese architect Kisho Kurokawa is enmeshed in a complicated philosophical nexus where architecture, futurism, societal instability, Buddhist notions of time and space, and a host of other ideas intermingle. His design for the Ehime Prefectural Museum of General Science is one of the latest in a series of buildings that attempt to give form to this evolving philosophy, which Kurokawa simply describes as an approach to architecture that encompasses the Japanese culture's implicit awareness of impermanence and perpetual change. More specifically, about this museum he says, "Architecture in a classical society is stable and permanent. Our society is dynamic, unstable. The design of the building refers to this reality." Today, it might be argued that there are no such classical societies.

Kurokawa works at producing a kind of unpredictability in his buildings; yet he is grounded and pragmatic, a successful, internationally renowned designer of enormous, multimillion dollar, complex structures—hotels, airport terminals, museums, and the like. Philosopher, master designer, and proprietor of a major architecture firm, Kurokawa remains personally responsible for every design his office produces. He does not delegate conceptual work, and he runs the office himself.

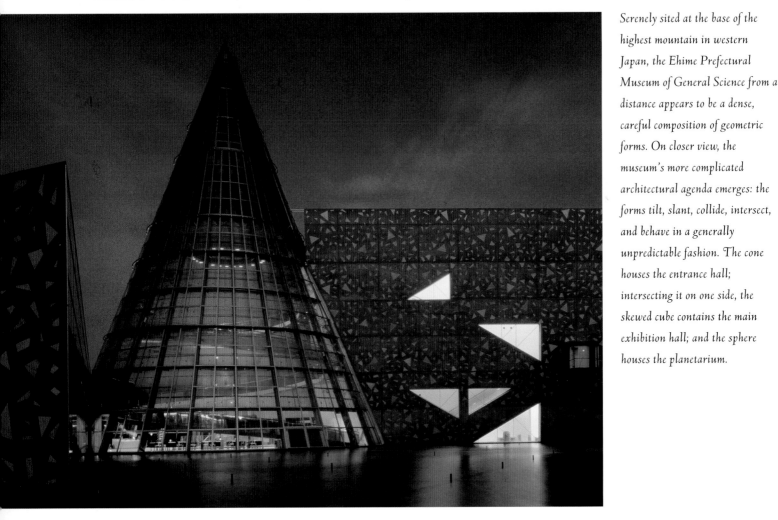

Serenely sited at the base of the highest mountain in western Japan, the Ehime Prefectural Museum of General Science from a distance appears to be a dense, careful composition of geometric forms. On closer view, the museum's more complicated architectural agenda emerges: the forms tilt, slant, collide, intersect, and behave in a generally unpredictable fashion. The cone houses the entrance hall; intersecting it on one side, the skewed cube contains the main exhibition hall; and the sphere houses the planetarium.

All photos by Tomio Ohashi

The education hall, right, exhibition hall, left, and outdoor exhibition space, foreground, show the interplay of geometric forms from differing angles. The freestanding triangular structure (below) serves as the museum's parking garage.

The museum is located in the suburb of Niihama on Shikoku Island, at the foot of the highest mountain in western Japan, in an area proximate to the future site of a major highway interchange. As is true with many of Kurokawa's projects, the complex consists of a grouping of distinct, easily recognizable geometric forms, but each time the architect puts these elements into play, something original emerges. In this case, the forms include a cone, a crescent, a cube, a square, and a triangle, arrayed in a pattern meant to evoke the random yet somehow precise arrangement of stepping stones in a Japanese garden. Thus, the refined asymmetry that is a Japanese cultural tradition is given another, larger meaning. Kurokawa uses the tradition to make an argument about the unsettled, unpredictable state of the world—an argument that is neatly counterpointed by the orderly presence of the built forms.

In this way, the architect repeatedly undermines the ostensible logic of his formal components. While the glowing glass cone of the museum's entrance hall fulfills its logical role as the focal, organizational volume and the orb of the planetarium likewise expresses its function through its form, there is a conscious effort at unpredictability underlying many aspects of the complex. The museum's square exhibition hall, for example, is skewed and tilted, and finished with four different exterior surfaces, composed of aluminum, glass, and exposed concrete. The relationship between the planetarium and the entrance hall is a secret one, expressed by the presence of a passage linking them that runs underground, beneath the pond that lies between them. On the exterior, asymmetrical fenestration, slanting planes, and metal triangles cast here and there into concrete surfaces undermine the sense of predictability. Inside, randomly patterned floor tiles, oddly angled wall and roof planes, and irregular door handles further the idea of instability.

Despite all this, the site plan is perfectly cohesive and logical, and the museum functions efficiently. Circulation zones are appropriately lively and easy to find and follow. There are contemplative places to rest, and the wide, shallow pond that lies at the heart of the complex provides soothing contrast to the dynamic interplay of the buildings. Kurokawa uses buildings as abstract symbols and tools for philosophical exploration, and yet, as this striking complex demonstrates, they are always clear, functional, and beautiful.

These views of the planetarium over the restaurant, and the mountains framed by the planetarium and the exhibition hall (seen from the restaurant interior) demonstrate the architect's capacity for creating soothing, contemplative spaces and beautifully composed views in the context of his edge-pushing collisions of forms and relationships.

Concrete imbedded with titanium plates makes a compelling surface finish; unpredictable locations and shapes for doors and windows add to the atmosphere of instability and impermanence sought by the architect.

Demonstrating that this very philosophical architect understands the fundamental need for grand gestures, particularly in the arrival sequence, the breathtaking interior volume of the entrance hall cone is washed by daylight through transparent walls. A view directly upward into the cone reveals a mandala-like symmetry.

Circulation corridors and exhibition spaces illustrate a commitment to sharpness of detailing and finish and well-balanced lighting, counterpointed by random tile patterns in the floor, unexpected angles in ceilings and walls, and strangely configured doorways and window openings. The mix of clarity and unpredictability is exhilarating.

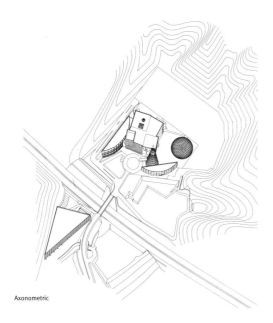

Axonometric

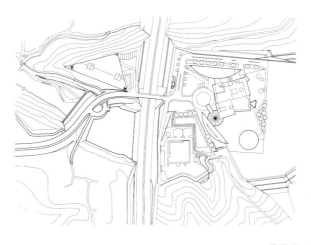

Site Plan

Axonometric view and site plan show the assemblage of geometric forms, with the triangular parking structure across the roadway at bottom left in axonometric view, top left in site plan.

Arizona Science Center
Phoenix, Arizona
Antoine Predock Architect

EARTHLY SCIENCE

Antoine Predock's rugged, sculptural assemblages of natural forms have earned him a place on that short list of American architects whose work might be described as visionary. Though many of his projects are located on nondescript boulevards in the sprawling cities of the American West— Phoenix, Las Vegas, Albuquerque—he has always looked beyond the city's edge, to the primeval vastness of the sky, mountain, and desert for inspiration. Thus, his buildings often are graced with a timelessness that transcends the mundane quality of their immediate surroundings.

Completed in 1997, the Arizona Science Center is situated on a busy street in Phoenix, surrounded by multiple, context-making structures: the historic houses of Heritage Square, a pedestrian shopping district, commercial warehouses, a large-scale civic center, a symphony hall, a history museum, and a park. A sports stadium will also be erected in the vicinity, adding another structure to the mix. All of these elements together shape an effort to transcend the culture of the car that has long dominated almost every western city, to create a pedestrian-friendly, urban neighborhood.

All photos by Timothy Hursley

The museum is a composition of abstracted natural forms drawn from the desert and built in an urban context. The monumental, aluminum-clad wedge serves as the unifying element and as backdrop for the other forms, including the octagonal planetarium. Myriad plazas, terraces, and staircases serve as gathering places around the building exterior.

Basic building materials—concrete and glass—are interwoven with open space to dissolve the boundaries between inside and outside. The monumentality of the forms suggests the vastness of the desert, mountains, and sky. The underground lobby (top) is bathed in banded light from openings in a stepped roof.

The windowless Science Center is composed of concrete knit into a massive but graceful assemblage of peaks, plateaus, hills, and buttes—a muscular abstraction of natural desert forms, shaped into a sculpture dominated by a tall, aluminum-clad wedge thrusting skywards. With this powerful peak serving as backdrop and unifying element, the museum is a strikingly dramatic piece when seen from outside and from afar.

Closer in, Predock has created what he describes as a "processional and participatory journey, beginning with a descent into the coolness of the earth at the entry courtyard." This journey into the earth leaves the city behind. Visitors may admire the sky, stretching over the sunken entry court; then, passing the store and cafe, they arrive at the museum itself via an orientation space located underground. From here, a wide corridor leads to stairs and paths linking exhibition galleries and theaters located within the cool confines of those abstract, geologically inspired forms that read so powerfully from the outside. As one would expect, considering that they are built inside "mountains," these volumes are vast: the theater's screen is five stories high, and there are five exhibition halls, two that are 12,500 square feet (1,125 square meters) in size, and three that are 2,500 square feet (225 square meters). After experiencing the myriad exhibitions in these spacious caverns, visitors eventually ascend to the roof atop the aluminum wedge, where an octagonal "star court" allows them to celebrate the great outdoors, and the vastness of the cosmos.

Appealing to many are the building's easily accessible exterior features: entry court steps, shaded decks, bleacher seats, and layered terraces that extend the museum into the adjacent park. Although these external gestures to some extent establish the museum in its urban place, the building's real "context" is out there in the hills.

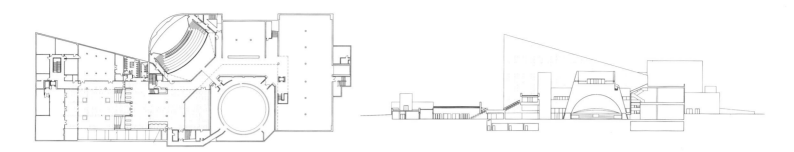

First-Floor Plan

East-West Section

The museum's galleries and
theaters are over-scale, windowless
volumes. High ceilings permit
dramatic, large-scale exhibitions,
while the theater ceiling provides
a cosmic glow.

Route 66 Museum
Clinton, Oklahoma
Elliott + Associates Architects

ROAD TO THE PROMISED LAND

Route 66 occupies a sweet spot in the collective unconscious of America. Simply say the two words and everybody hears the tune, recalls the television show, sees flashing neon reflecting in a silvery mirage atop a shimmering two-lane blacktop, a Route 66 road sign poised like a sentinel on a desert shoulder. Pick your decade, your make of car, and "get your kicks." Completed in 1932, the 2,400-mile, two-lane road passed through eight states en route from Chicago to LA. Lined with red Burma Shave signs, gas station outposts, concrete teepees, and quirky, dusty, little American towns, Route 66 was the road to the promised land, California.

A museum has been made to celebrate this legendary roadway. Located in Clinton, Oklahoma, a small town along the drive, the Route 66 Museum is the work of Oklahoma architect Rand Elliott, a sophisticated heartland modernist who has renovated, expanded, and decorated a roadside building to house this paean to the culture of the highway. The man was born in Clinton himself, so his attachment to the town is more than passing. The museum is multipurpose, according to Elliott: it is intended to explore the cultural impact of the highway by overviewing automobile and road-building technology, mixing academics and pop culture to study Oklahoma's Route 66 history; it also provides a forum for educational events and programs to promote the sense of the highway as a historic entity and to encourage tourism and preservation along the road itself.

The architect began with a 5,000-square-foot (450-square-meter), one-story Route 66 roadside structure that housed a rather nondescript operation called the Western Trails Museum. Elliott took this uninspired building, and rather than make it into something slick—"Route 66 is not about

The architect added the double-height, glass-block-walled addition, pinkish-tinged glass-block columns, roof fins, neon arrow, and some racy signage to transform a drab little one-story roadside building into the gaudy, eye-catching Route 66 Museum in Clinton, Oklahoma, on the original Route 66. The first-seen exhibit, contained inside the glass wall out front, is the ultimate Route 66 machine: a Corvette convertible. Visitors have likened the building to a restaurant, a drive-in theater, and a curio shop—ideal inhabitants of the commercial American Main Street that was Route 66.

All photos by Robert W. Shimer, Hedrich-Blessing

slick buildings," he says—he expanded it while dressing it up in roadside flash: lighted columns and glass block with hot-red neon signage on a double-height facade, with the sides shingled in black and gray stripes. The original building is still there, it's just been dolled-up in the finest tradition of Route 66, where you could find all manner of garish pop-culture "architecture" thrown up in a brazen attempt to catch the eye of drivers flying past at 50 or 60 miles (80 or 96 kilometers) an hour. The museum has been likened to a restaurant, a drive-in theater, and a curio shop; these words are music to Elliott's ears, who calls his hometown baby "a cross between a cheap bar and a motel."

Nevertheless, it is a museum, and the visitor's experience has been orchestrated to explore the Route 66 story in an orderly fashion. The interior is organized as a circulation loop, around which visitors will travel. The first exhibition area, the aptly nicknamed Wow Room, is an out-thrusting, glass-enclosed space that looks like an auto showroom; with a

vintage Corvette (alternating with a '56 Thunderbird) on display ready to hit the highway, this is the showroom of on-the-road dreams. Beyond this opening zinger, exhibits are organized around the motifs of automobiles, travel, words and phrases from the early Route 66 era, and artifacts and imagery from world events and pop culture of the time. With a big, pink, curio cabinet stuffed with cheap, roadside trinkets, a late-1960s psychedelic VW bus, steel trusses that recall the bridges along the way, and a 1950s diner, among other elements, the interior mingles architecture, exhibition, and artifacts into a lively, interactive experience. Rand Elliott says, "We don't have our Whitneys or our Guggenheims out here. What we have is a renegade, outlaw kind of tradition—a rich, interesting history, and Route 66 is part of that." This museum is wonderfully evocative, an inspired example of how to transform the detritus of pop-culture and local history into a sentimental journey that entertains and enlightens.

The architect finished the sides of the double-height addition with black and gray shingles in a striped pattern. Glass-block columns added to the front of the original building link the new and old.

The steel truss system in the upper reaches of the double-height addition is designed after bridges along Route 66.

The big, pink, curio cabinet is filled with roadside junk and memorabilia. These gaudy, mass-produced, and eccentric artifacts exert a powerful nostalgic appeal.

The diner doesn't serve food, but the mix of authentic and reproduced furniture, accessories, and finishes effortlessly evokes the 1950s. The car is a mint-condition 1952 Ford sedan.

Papalote Children's Museum
Mexico City, Mexico
Legorreta Arquitectos

A GARDEN OF GEOMETRIC DELIGHTS

Situated on the edge of Chapultepec Park west of downtown Mexico City, the Papalote (it means *kite*) Children's Museum forms a kind of border for the park and its forest, with fountains and gardens that integrate the museum topography into the natural environs of the park. The flowing waters of the Guadalupe River in the park are also symbolically linked via water features with the museum's interior courtyard, heightening the connection to nature. The sense of integration into the natural world is ultimately expressed via the open, accessible atmosphere of the museum—an atmosphere evoked by a free-flowing relationship of inside to outside, by spacious gardens and patios, by a main building with multiple setbacks to lessen its mass, with much of the interior illumination provided by high skylights.

The buildings and grounds and the interactive exhibits within are intended to evoke in children the sense of liberation and exploration that an immersion into nature awakens. This is no easy task in Mexico City, one of the most crowded urban environments in the world. As if to balance, or at least minimally negate, the complicated harshness of the city, the museum is deliberately simple and nonintimidating; as Legorreta notes, when children are in the building, "they should feel as if the museum belongs exclusively to them."

All photos by Lourdes Legorreta

The low-rise museum complex is composed of several separate, distinct volumes in basic geometric forms and bright, appealing colors, making it easily recognized and remembered by children. The project is extensively landscaped, creating literal and symbolic links with Chapultepec Park. The sphere contains interactive exhibits, and the yellow wedge is an IMAX theater, the roof of which is an open-air performance space.

The bright-yellow entrance is flanked by stone-clad and purple columns supporting a wedge-shaped, shade-making pavilion. The waiting line for tickets is defined by low walls painted in the same bright yellow. Colorful tile cladding enlivens building exteriors and evokes Mexico's handicraft traditions.

To achieve this, the museum's distinct buildings and forms are composed in simple, immediately recognizable shapes—spheres, rectangles, pyramids, wedges, cylinders—and invitingly bold colors. Casting an ancient Mexican tradition in a lively contemporary mold, the architects clad the buildings' exteriors in glazed color tiles, making a finish that educates, by exploring this timeless craft, and yet is joyful, childlike. The entire complex is composed in this manner, with the educational elements gently layered on. Without being heavy-handed, why not teach Mexican children about their country's marvelously rich craft tradition?

Playfully patterned or applied in warm, primary colors, these tiles lend a vibrant quality to the complex, one that is naturally appealing to children. Children also find irresistible the round sandbox wrapped around an enormous yellow column (a relic from the factory that used to occupy the site), with a swooping fabric shade stretched overhead like a ship's sail. These colors and shapes say, "Come play." The sculpted, blue-and-green dinosaur in the garden says, "Come play and learn." Children will come to play—and to learn, for everything here is designed to make them feel that this is their place.

Playful sculptures, play areas, and water features in enclosed courtyards—a tradition in many Mexican buildings—establish a link with the natural environment of neighboring Chapultepec Park.

Though the complex lies within the intensely urban environs of Mexico City, the site plan and the elevation show how the museum's differing volumes are intermingled with gardens and courtyards to enhance the relationship with the nearby park. In plan, the entry is at center, to the right of the sphere, with the IMAX and open-air theaters stacked to the left and the main museum, courtyard display, and play areas to the right.

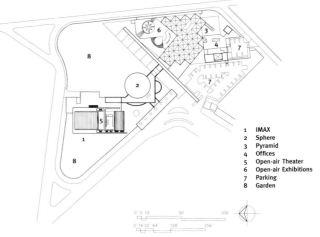

1 IMAX
2 Sphere
3 Pyramid
4 Offices
5 Open-air Theater
6 Open-air Exhibitions
7 Parking
8 Garden

Site Plan

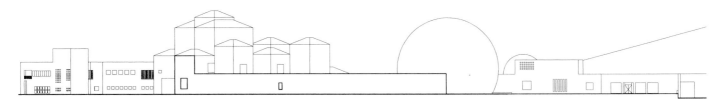

Elevation

Bathed in natural light from skylights set high in pyramid-shaped ceilings, the interior galleries are wonderfully colorful, exciting spaces, filled with interactive exhibits meant to be both educational and entertaining.

Vitra Design Museum
Weil am Rheim, Basel, Switzerland
Frank O. Gehry and Associates, Inc.

ART CONTAINING ARTIFACTS

Given architect Frank Gehry's long involvement with the art world, his evolution as a builder of museums would seem inevitable—and his progress has made compelling architectural theater. After completing several museum projects in the Los Angeles area, he moved on to a larger stage: the Vitra Design Museum near Basel, Switzerland was one of his first overseas projects to garner international acclaim. Gehry's commission included both the museum, designed to house a collection of chairs belonging to Vitra's owner, and a new wing for the chair company's factory. Positioned out front to serve as a gateway to the factory complex, the museum shares elements with the new Gehry-designed factory wing directly behind it. Here as never before, the architect composed a structure that is more sculpture than building, or is rather a sculpted building, its exterior form gracefully assembled out of distinct volumes in a pattern that on casual inspection appears almost random.

Gehry's artistic/architectural aim is remarkably true, despite the chances he takes. These fragments—spirals, wedges, cubes, crosses—cohere to form a harmonious structure. Remarkably, for all its ostensibly chaotic qualities—buildings are not supposed to look like icebergs afloat on a sea of grass!—this riveting, gleaming white edifice is possessed of an altogether dignified mien, generated by the purity of the white plaster exterior counterpointed with selectively applied titanium. This is all made true by the finesse with which Gehry balances his voluptuous assemblage of interlocking volumes to make a whole.

The meaning of these shapes on the exterior emerges as they are seen from within. They enclose staircases, or vaulted galleries, or sweeping, canopied ceilings over exhibit areas. Essentially the interior display areas are open, with enclosed offices confined to one side, thus they are fairly

All photos by Thomas Dix

Architect Frank Gehry's cubist assemblage of interlocking forms makes a somewhat chaotic initial impression, but this view of the entry facade reveals the building's underlying symmetry. A cruciform skylight (at top center) daylights the interior. Visible at rear right, a piece of the factory building also designed by Frank Gehry. The two structures are architecturally harmonious.

easy to read: from the entry one accesses a temporary exhibition space beneath a cruciform skylight, set on angle into the central roof two stories above. The cruciform glazed opening provides extensive natural illumination for the unconfined, free-flowing galleries on both floors. A stair curves off the entry lobby; a second spirals up from a perimeter display area at rear. The second-level display areas surround the floor-to-ceiling opening at the heart of the interior, beneath the skylight. Natural wood, concrete, or gray-carpeted floors provide a stable base for the display and observation platforms, the chairs that form the collection, the unexpected twists and turns in the walls, and the dynamic ceiling lines and planes— planes that bring the cubist jazz of the exterior to the interior, injecting the space with boundless energy. This could have been an opportunity to create a safe, understated box for this fine bunch of chairs. Instead, Gehry cut loose in his unpredictable yet ultimately disciplined fashion. This piece of architecture is art.

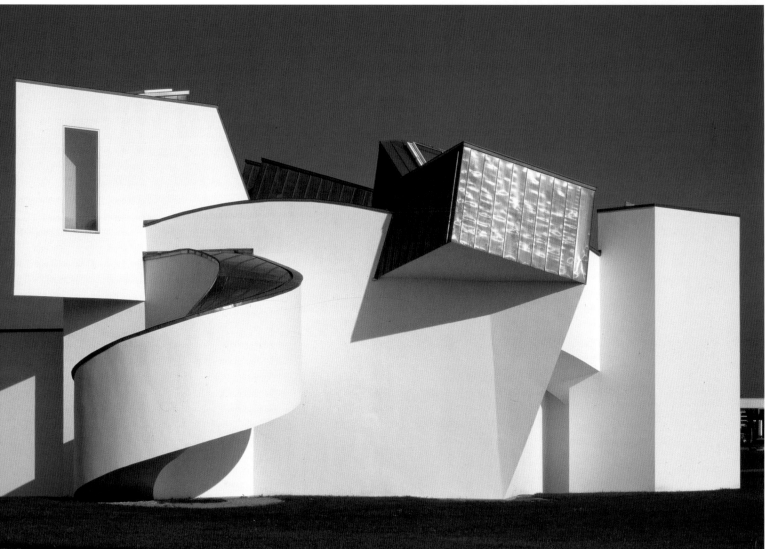

Views of the building's exterior illustrate the graceful interplay of geometric volumes, curving lines, angles, and planes. White painted plaster and titanium finishes lend the building a certain dignity. The visual impression of the museum shifts with the point of view, but the audaciously original form of the sculpted structure is always utterly compelling.

Interior views (below, opposite, and previous page) of assorted special exhibitions and permanent collection displays show how the gallery areas on both floors are left open, so that everything flows together. Daylight from multiple skylights illuminates both levels, supplemented with artificial lighting as needed. The myriad angles, niches, and intersections of the walls and ceilings bring some of the exterior's cubist dynamic inside, but the quiet finishes— white walls, gray concrete and carpet, and natural wood floors— provide a neutral envelope for the furniture and the lively backdrops employed to display it.

Chikatsu-Asuka Historical Museum
Osaka, Japan
Tadao Ando Architect & Associates

ANCESTRAL SANCTUARY

Chikatsu-Asuka in the southern region of the Osaka prefecture played an important role in Japan's earliest historical period, between the fourth and seventh centuries, and thus is home to one of the country's most extensive collections of burial mounds, or *kofun*. There are over two hundred such mounds at Chikatsu, including four imperial tombs. In order to preserve, study, and exhibit these fascinating remnants of early Japanese culture, the Osaka prefecture commissioned Tadao Ando to design a museum that would be integrated with the burial mounds at the site and also provide an overview.

Ando responded with a museum design that utilizes a stepped hill of plain concrete rising from the natural terrain as its primary architectural element, which will provide visitors with views of the entire burial mound group as well as plum trees, a nearby pond, and paths weaving amongst the surrounding hills. The main interior of the museum is sunken partially into the earth and enclosed beneath this man-made hill, which is essentially a slanting roof consisting of hundreds of wide, shallow steps that rise to flow around a concrete tower wrapped with a staircase. The tower rises starkly, a blocky, windowless monument signifying the solemn presence of a history museum with an emphasis on cultural artifacts associated with death and burial. And yet, the dynamic sweep of the steps, the platform atop the tower, and level plazas at the summit of the steps all serve as outdoor gathering spaces, transforming the exterior of the museum into a place for celebrations and festivals. According to the architect, the plaza will be used to stage musical and dramatic performances as well as lectures and readings.

Aerial view shows the museum in its entirety, a pale monument etched in stark contrast against the green, rural site amidst a scattering of over two hundred ancient burial mounds. The museum's primary volume lies beneath a man-made hill of steps that is also a roof rising from ground level. A solemn windowless tower lifts from the roof, providing a higher perspective from which visitors can view the pond, hills, and burial mounds.

Photo by Mitsuo Matsuoka

Views from the bottom of the hill of steps and from across the pond. The spare, unadorned finish takes on a soft, golden glow in late afternoon light. A blocky, windowless tower is an appropriately stark monument to crown a museum devoted to gathering and studying the artifacts of death and burial. The smaller block at right contains a skylight over a lightwell that reaches three stories down to form a courtyard on the basement level of the museum.

Photos by Shigeo Ogawa

The finishes of the exterior materials contrast sharply with the surrounding greenery, but these tough, raw materials possess a malleable quality, depending on the changing daylight for their color. The myriad ramps, angles, and differing segments of the enormous, complex stair system create an intriguing contrast of geometric forms with the unpredictable shapes that trails and streams take on as they are shaped by geography, weather, and time on the surrounding hills. So, though it stands nobly, solemnly apart, Ando's small yet monumental man-made mountain is integrated into the hilly terrain.

The interior of the museum is entered near the top, so visitors must ascend the hill—thus taking in the views—to descend into the three levels of the interior, likened by architect Ando to a tomb. The display areas, reaching deeply into space carved out beneath the steps, are kept dark intentionally, to foster the grave atmosphere, and the objects on display are arrayed as they were discovered in the nearby tombs. Ando's interiors are always spatially complex yet functionally clear, composed of the simplest materials; this natural wood, concrete, and glass interior is consistent with that history. Wrapped around a skylight-topped void that reaches to the basement level to form an inner courtyard, the interiors include, along with permanent and temporary exhibition galleries organized by subject matter and chronology, a cafe, a library/workshop, an auditorium, a photo studio, offices, and storage and work areas. In a sense, the interiors are of secondary importance in this site-specific museum, with its emphasis on plazas, outward views, and connections with the terrain. Nevertheless, both inside and out, Ando has evoked an appropriate sense of timelessness as well as conveying the profound respect this culture has for its past and for its dead.

Views of the lightwell that reaches from its glass skylight crown down to the basement level, where a replica of the Rokutaniji Tower at the Rokutan Temple has been placed in a square inner courtyard. A slanting ramp crosses the lightwell on the first level above the courtyard. Natural wood floors offer a warming counterpoint to the minimally textured concrete finishes.

Photos by Shigeo Ogawa and Tadao Ando

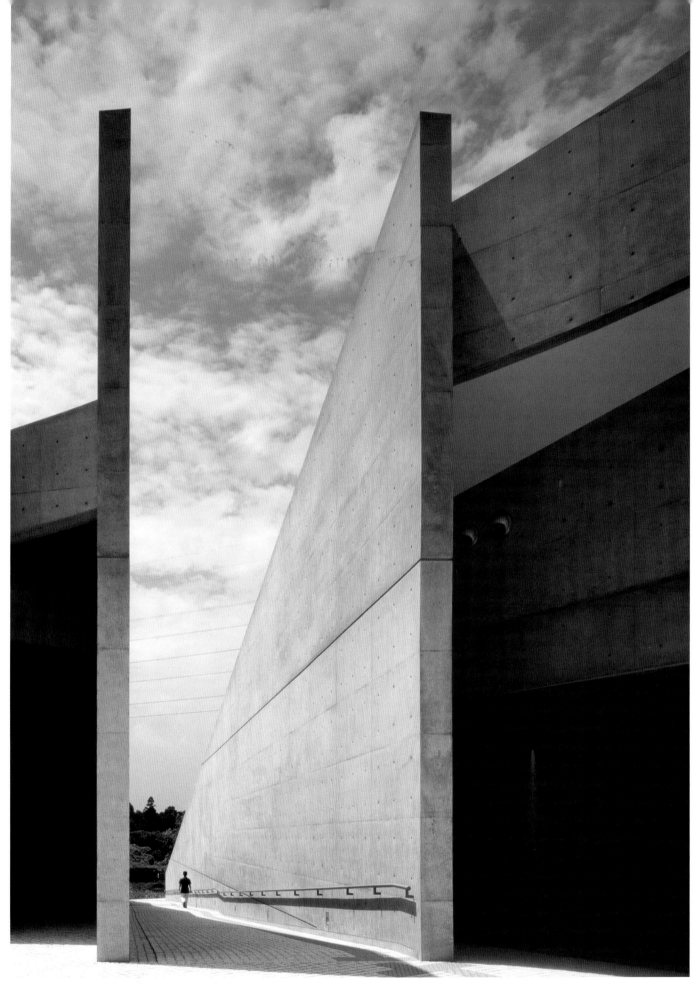

This ramp slices through the stepped hill on an angle, carving out a deep passage that gives a perspective of the fairly monumental scale of the hill that houses the museum. The project illustrates the austere beauty to be found in simple, minimally adorned materials.

Photo by Shigeo Ogawa

Site plan shows burial-mound
remnants drawn in to the right.

Photo by Tadao Ando

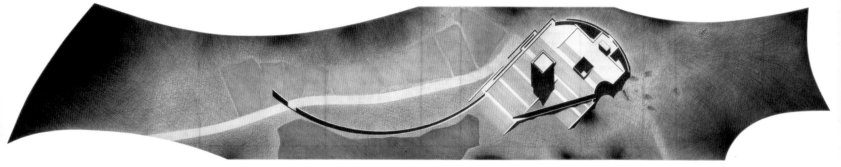

Site Plan

The museum is positioned in a
small valley with a pond at the base
of the stepped hill that forms the roof.

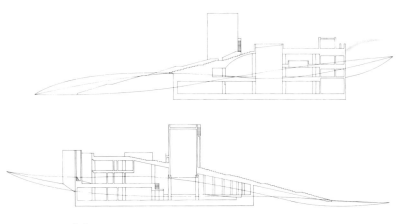

Sections

Sections illustrate the way the
building is both carved into the
terrain and raised above it, with a
sloped roof composed of steps. The
basement-level exhibition space
reaches deeply under the steps, and
the tower is sunken below the
artificial grade. The walls
enclosing the inner courtyard
beneath the skylight articulate a
volume that is the same as that of
the tower.

The museum's largest permanent exhibition space is this circular gallery on the basement level, where relics and objects (called haniwa) excavated from nearby tombs have been positioned in a dramatic circle around the lowered central display area. The keyhole-shaped object at center is a model of the Nintokuryo Tumulus, one of the largest imperial tombs in the world. This gallery is located almost entirely underneath the hill of steps that comprises the major portion of the museum's roof. The light is kept low to evoke the atmosphere of a tomb.

Photo by Shigeo Ogawa

Nariwa Museum
Nariwa, Okayama, Japan
Tadao Ando Architect & Associates

THE POETRY OF EMPTY SPACE

Tadao Ando's poetic minimalism is remarkably flexible and expressive. Repeatedly he shifts and rearranges the most basic materials and forms—concrete, glass, and water, rectangles, cubes, and other fundamental shapes and volumes—and with subtle attention to the interplay of scale and site, creates structures that rest tranquilly in their locations. His buildings effortlessly evoke the kind of serenity associated with the most elegant and spare of Japanese gardens. He is a master of manipulating emptiness, finding and focusing the quiet beauty that lies at the heart of contained space.

Intended to house art and artifacts related to the Nariwa area, a prosperous region known for its copper mines, the Nariwa Museum is a quintessential Ando building stripped down to the basics, constructed primarily of concrete and glass, with steel details and wood floors. The museum is delicately positioned between the site of an old residence surrounded by a stone wall, and a steep hill. Ando placed another layer of wall within the existing stone wall and then put a concrete box within it.

Visitors approaching from the parking area first encounter the original stone wall, which anchors the building in its historic context, and then ascend an angled ramp that winds around part of the perimeter and slices through the concrete and glass cubes containing the museum's various spaces. With the insertion of this single diagonal ramp, the architect transforms myriad interior and exterior volumes from simple boxes to more eccentrically angular spaces. Within the structure, along with a cafe, a shop, storage area, and other office and back-of-house areas, a series of single- and double-height galleries and exhibition areas on two levels are counterpointed by walled, roofless voids. On the exterior, a generously proportioned water surface lies between the building and the nearby slope. Between water and building, exterior stairs, sections of walls, and terraces make space that links inside and outside. Expanses of glass and varied openings in the building further enhance the sense that this is, in Ando's words, "a place where nature, culture, and history come together."

The Nariwa Museum is contained within layered walls of natural finished concrete. A large expanse of water links the building to a steep, tree-covered incline nearby.

A sloping ramp, terraces, and outdoor stairs enhance the connection of the museum interior to the natural world.

By making roofless outdoor rooms both inside and outside the museum's natural concrete walls, Ando frames expanses of nature— sky, trees, water—thereby making them part of the museum-going experience.

Photos by Mitsuo Matsuoka

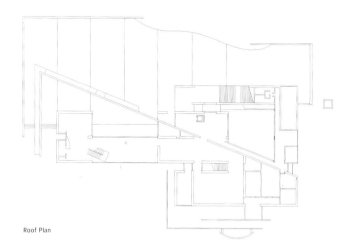

Roof Plan

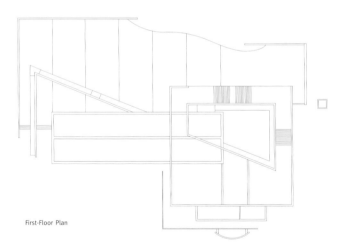

Second-Floor Plan

Two views of a long, double-height gallery illustrate the powerful beauty inherent in minimalist architecture. Glass walls heighten the relationship of inside to outside.

Photos by Mitsuo Matsuoka and Tadao Ando

First-Floor Plan

Plans show how the insertion of a single diagonal element alters the internal logic of the architecture, creating assorted angular volumes. A ramp on the outside of the diagonal provides visual access to the pool at top while directing visitors into the museum. The roof plan reveals the areas that are contained within the museum walls, but open to the sky.

Photo on facing page by Shigeo Ogawa

A FUSION OF PAST AND PRESENT

The McCord Museum consists of the original 1906 building at left (the original entrance is around the corner at far left) and the newer structure at right, with a gridded-glass link set back between both. Though the new wing is unmistakably modern in its sparely decorated clarity, the similarity in color of the limestone, the matching scale of window openings, and the metal details, evident in the storefront-style, street-level windows, serve to fuse the two into one. Vertical openings in the new wing signal the location and height of new exhibition galleries.

All photos by Michel Brunelle

The McCord Museum in Montreal, Quebec, is an urban museum with a quirky, historical collection amassed by a wealthy Montreal attorney, David Ross McCord, in the late nineteenth and early twentieth centuries. McCord's collection, an odd, scholarly, and personal treasure trove of immigrant and Native American artifacts, is housed in a six-story limestone palazzo with its primary facade fronting busy Sherbrooke Street adjacent to McGill University. Designed in 1906 by Montreal architect Percy Nobbs as a student union, the handsome building suffered the indignity of being completely gutted in 1971, when the McCord collection was installed. At that time the architects stripped the interiors, blocked the windows, and built featureless 1970s-style black-box exhibition spaces. (The black box was a short-lived deviation from the primary display space trend of the last fifty years, the white box.) Given the eclectic nature of the McCord holdings—Native American beadwork and canoe paddles, a bill of fare from a Masonic dinner in 1841, a prayer book translated into Mohawk, burnt sticks from an explorer's campfire, and eighty thousand other items amassed over the lifetime of an obsessive collector—in retrospect, this design choice makes clear the perils of chasing architectural trends. This material does not fit into black boxes.

In the late 1980s the private museum's governing board commissioned the Montreal firm of LeMoyne Lapointe Magne (in association with JLP Architects) to renovate and expand the McCord. The architects responded with a judicious, modest design firmly planted in the modern age while paying all due respect to the museum's historical roots. They added a 55,400-square-foot (4,986-square-meter) contemporary addition to the south of the original building that complements the existing exterior by utilizing limestone of a similar tone, a tripartite facade punctuated with window openings that match the scale of the original, and bronze details that recall the older mullions without copying them. Set back from both elevations, a gridded glass wall joins them, flooding the interior with light and creating a view (in an otherwise understated facade) into the new four-story secondary entrance and stairwell on quiet Victoria Street, around the corner from the original Sherbrooke Street entry foyer. A curving copper roof provides another link between the two wings.

The new four-story stairwell and entry on the west side of the building is balanced by a three-story interior court on the east side. Wrapped around a 35-foot-high (10.7-meter-high) Haida totem pole, the new stairs provide the main access route to the new large-scale exhibition galleries on the second and third floors.

The focal point in the west entry is a new staircase that serves as the primary access route to upper-level galleries; the stair is designed around a 35-foot-high (10.7-meter-high) Haida totem pole. On the east side of the building, a three-story interior courtyard counterpoints the four-story entry space. With these light-giving volumes as anchors, the architects created two spacious, flexible galleries on the second and third stories in the new wing. The galleries share an elevator core and light well, and walkways linking them span the volumes of the stairwell and the interior courtyard on each floor, enhancing the north-south circulation axis emanating from the Sherbrooke Street entrance. On the fourth floor, in the original wing, a grand ballroom that had been divided into two levels of mini-galleries has had its high-ceilinged glory restored, albeit with a new purpose: creating a lofty, stack-lined reading room and research center. The fifth floor is reserved for offices, meeting rooms, storage, and other functional space.

Throughout the structure, a consistent materials palette, including slate, glass, maple, concrete, and gray steel, deepens the connections between old and new, as does a continuous floorplate, seamlessly linking original to renovation on every level. By concentrating the larger, flexible galleries in the new wing and the smaller, intimate galleries housing prints, paintings, costumes, and textiles in the more formal original building, each wing is given its own identity.

Foregoing the flash and commercial appeal of many modern museums, this project takes a more conservative tack. The architects have done a graceful job of renewing the building without diminishing the urbane qualities that originally distinguished it.

Walkways span both east and west volumes on the second and third floors.

On the ground floor, this curving counter can be found in the museum's restaurant/bar, close to the original and primary entrance. The passage leads to the new three-story interior courtyard on the east side of the building. Utilized throughout the building, cost-effective materials include slate, gray-painted steel, glass, concrete, and maple, installed selectively to add a hint of richness.

The grand ballroom in the original building has been transformed into a reading room and research center.

Located in the older Percy Nobbs-designed wing, this renovated gallery demonstrates the virtue of displaying antique pieces—furniture, portraiture, etc.—in clean, modern surroundings. These are but a scant few of the McCord Collection's more than eighty thousand pieces.

This elevation drawing shows the balance of similarity and difference between the original building, left, and the addition, right. A continuous roofline binds them, while a gridded-glass wall separates and joins.

URBAN ARCHAEOLOGY

The Montreal firm of LeMoyne Lapointe Magne approaches the aged buildings they work on with respect tempered by a decidedly contemporary attitude: they excavate, reveal, and ultimately celebrate the makings of these old structures by boldly juxtaposing the modern against the original. One never doubts which is which, yet both new and old are brought into sharper focus.

Constructed in 1837, renovated in 1881 and again in the 1970s, the neoclassical Old Custom House more recently has been transformed into a gift shop and auxiliary exhibition space for Montreal's museum of archaeology and history.

All photos by Michel Brunelle

Montreal's Old Custom House, renovated and transformed in the early 1990s into an auxiliary exhibition space and gift shop for the adjacent Point à Callière archaeology and history museum, is a quintessential expression of this attitude. The Old Custom House is a 6,000-square-foot (540-square-meter) neoclassical building erected in 1837 by twenty-five-year-old architect John Ostell, who later became famous for his Notre Dame Basilica nearby. In 1881, the southern St. Lawrence river facade of the Old Custom House was taken apart and moved closer to the river to make room for a 3,000-square-foot (270-square-meter) addition. In spite of this, by 1919 the building had been outgrown. A new customs house was built several blocks away, and the old one was turned into an office annex that eventually suffered a destructive 1970s renovation.

The Old Custom House now rests atop one end of an enormous archaeological excavation, a section of the museum designed literally to expose Montreal history back to the pre-immigrant days when the Iroquois had a settlement on the site. The last section of this vast crypt contains the Old Custom House foundations, excavated by LeMoyne Lapointe Magne. From the crypt, museum-goers ascend into the new Old Custom House. With a gift shop on premises, the venerable structure now serves as a kind of coda to the museum tour.

Cutting back two 1970s-era concrete floors to the point at which the 1837 facade once stood, the architects excavated, exposing the southern section of the interior from cellar to roof, creating an enormous void and revealing original limestone walls, window openings, and wooden roof beams, in a sense thereby letting the building tell its own story. Replacing the rotten beams with concrete, the architects opened up a cellar adjacent to the crypt and installed an exhibition on the building's history in this subterranean space.

Steel walkways bridge the expansive volume the architects created by taking out concrete floors to open the building from cellar to roof. They also peeled back layers of renovation to expose original limestone walls and deep window openings. The cylinder that partially wraps the elevator shaft is meant to echo waterfront grain elevators or the smokestack of a steamship.

In the conceptual scheme, the architects relate the 1881 addition to the port lying to the south, and thus a cylindrical elevator shaft echoes a steamship smokestack or a grain elevator such as those along the riverfront. Mezzanines on the first and second stories allow enhanced visual access to the dramatic, triple-height volume. In the earliest, circa-1837 northern section of the building—a section conceptually related to the city to the north—a more orderly set of new rooms contain the gift shop on the first floor and permanent exhibitions on the second. In both sections, the architects made clean, contemporary walkways, railings, and stairs out of steel, with perforated metal employed to screen mechanical ducts. A spiral stair is also made out of contemporary steel, rendering in new fashion a form that recalls the spiral fire stairs of nineteenth-century Montreal apartment buildings. This modern rendition of a traditional element is typical of the firm's approach to renovation and restoration; its graceful lines are a fitting demonstration of the value to be found in enriching the old by making it new.

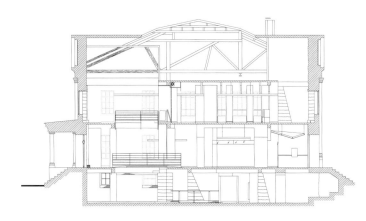

Section

Section and plans show great space created by opening the floors towards the front of the building at bottom. Exhibit areas occupy the | *basement and upper levels, with mezzanines surrounding the central void on the first and second levels.*

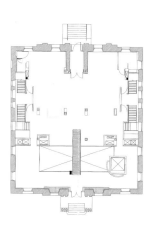

Basement Plan

First-Floor Plan

Second-Floor Plan

Cellar-level gallery juxtaposes new and old: steel railings and flooring against ancient limestone and brick.

A rather sleek spiral stair on the upper level demonstrates the architects' penchant for using contemporary interpretations of traditional forms. Similar stairs were often employed as fire escapes on nineteenth-century Montreal apartment buildings.

United States Holocaust Memorial Museum
Washington, D.C.
Pei Cobb Freed & Partners

IN REMEMBRANCE

The palpable, almost unbearable tension that cleaves to this striking building is no accident. Architect James Ingo Freed set out to express the horror of the Holocaust in his design for a memorial to the six million Jews slain in the Nazi death camps of the 1930s and 1940s. The tension is somewhat driven by the paradox of his success, for Freed has made a darkly beautiful building to commemorate this monumentally evil passage in history. Perhaps the most difficult architectural issues in the world are raised here: Is it right to make aesthetically satisfying architecture to educate people about the hideous truth of the Holocaust? And if so, down what path does the architect tread to attain that truth?

Freed has taken on these difficult concerns in creating the United States Holocaust Memorial Museum, adjacent to the Washington Mall. Seeking to learn more about the Holocaust as well as receive inspiration for the structure, Freed and the original director of the museum (Arthur Rosenblatt, author of this book's foreword) visited death camps in Poland, Austria, and Germany. What they discovered, and what emerged in the design of

The curving, limestone facade is a rather heavy-handed piece of neoclassicism, which nevertheless places the building in context among Washington D.C.'s many monumental structures. The curve pushes it out into the street beyond its neighbors, yet it is nothing more than facade, a mask for what lies behind.

On facing page: More than one thousand photographs of the members of the Jewish shtetl of Ejszyszki are displayed on canted, double-height walls in the north tower bridge. The village lies in what is now Lithuania. Most of the people pictured here perished in a single day, victims of the Nazis.

All photos by Timothy Hursley

the museum, was the awful efficiency and accessibility of the death camps. Technically modern, with the manufacturers' names proudly stamped on, the death-camp barracks, gas chambers, and crematoria were well-made examples of modern industrial architecture: this was the technology of a rational civilization that had morally disintegrated.

With its deliberate echoes of the warped efficiency of the camps, the museum embodies this disintegration. The entry facade on 14th Street is a heavy, curving limestone screen, almost completely detached from the building, its awkwardly wrought classicism putting it in context with the limestone neoclassicism of the Bureau of Engraving and Printing next door. To the north, four five-story brick towers evoke the guard towers of the death camps, while matching the Victorian red brick and rooflines of the other neighbor, the 1879 Auditor's Building.

Beyond the entry's three-story atrium lies the museum's central space, the Hall of Witness. Freed labels it a "resonator of memory, a stage for introspection, rather than as a series of specific architectural metaphors." With its oddly skewed, downward-pressing skylight spanning brick walls with diagonal steel bracing, it has a disquieting effect—as well it should, for it is within these daylit confines that visitors are moved from the placid environs of the Washington Mall toward a deeper understanding of the Holocaust. The rough brick walls echo the favored building material of the death camps; steel bracing was used on the crematorium ovens. In fact, throughout this unsettling space the interplay of forms, the construction practices, and every other element is deliberately chosen to echo Nazi architectural practices, to subtly evoke the technology of death.

Linked by stairs and glass block bridges that continually return visitors to the Hall of Witness, three floors of powerful exhibits—a reconstructed Auschwitz barracks, the photographic history of a single, annihilated Jewish town, a boxcar like those used to transport prisoners to the death camps—reveal the Holocaust in all its horror. The exhibits are arranged sequentially: the Nazi rise on the fourth floor, the Final Solution on the

third, and the aftermath on the second. A fifth floor with limited access is reserved for archives and research, while the concourse level contains theaters, classrooms, and conference space. In the end, visitors arrive at the Hall of Remembrance, a somber 6,000-square-foot (540-square-meter) hexagonal limestone volume that has been shaped to suggest the interior of an ancient tomb. Here, in soft illumination, visitors are invited to light memorial candles and contemplate the dead before exiting—a journey that will take them back through the Hall of Witness, with its ominous evocations of the death camps. After exploring the museum's exhibits, this space resonates even more deeply with both beauty and terror, a testament to the power of the architecture.